"Invaluable for anyone who reads or writes poetry, or has a restless desire of any kind, this wondrous, zany compendium gives us 'a biography of poetry' that directly enters our veins, bypassing all the crud and restoring our sense of the art, and David Meltzer is a champion of the impossible to have compiled it. Out of print since 1977, this new expanded edition is a gift of delight and wisdom—keep it in your bag by day and by your bed at night."—Mary Ruefle

"A great book of learning from a lifetime's thoughts of the poem. Ramble, scribble, tickle, lightbulb! Timely and highly worthwhile."—Clark Coolidge

"This heterogenous master volume is filled with advice, speculation, enthusiasm, new and ancient esoterica, play, collage, resistance, creative and useful definitions of major poetic terms, practical counsel about how to read and write poetry and so much more. All this makes it not only an idiosyncratic and welcome guide to reading and writing poetry, but also a kind of poem itself. Reading *Two-Way Mirror*, I feel continually surprised, excited, alive. This book makes me want to make poems, and readers, beware: if you are not already a poet, this book could very well turn you into one."—Matthew Zapruder

"This is a marvelously ingenious re-edition of a small classic with a fresh introduction, clever retro pictures, and a highly personal conclusion. Meltzer, one of the very last Beat poets still standing (and writing!) offers to young people in particular a provocative guide on how to think about becoming a poet and how to be a poet, drawing upon the transhistorical, shamanic wisdom and memory that are the poet's basic tools. *Two-Way Mirror* will be widely read and highly valued."—Paul Buhle

"David Meltzer had set out, when he was very young, to write a long poem called *The History of Everything*, an ambition that his later poetry brought ever closer to fulfillment. Here, in *Two-Way Mirror*, he shows us the underpinnings for such an enterprise: a brilliant & wise work as rich in insights & discoveries today as when it was first published in 1977. I know of no better amalgam of poetry & poetics & no better introduction to the ways in which poetry can emerge for us & lead us beyond ourselves & toward our own fulfillments. Meltzer's grace of mind & the life of poetry that surrounds it make the case complete."—Jerome Rothenberg

# TWO-WAY MIRROR

## The School

This great building is a school.

Boys and girls go to this school. They are strong boys and girls. Their mothers and fathers give them apples, eggs, butter and milk. These good foods keep them strong.

There are rooms in the school building. There are schools in New York and Washington.

---

NEW WORDS: school boys girls paper

---

# TWO-WAY MIRROR
## A Poetry Notebook

David Meltzer

City Lights San Francisco

Drawing of the author on p. 215 by Amanda Rose Meltzer

ACKNOWLEDGMENTS: "The word" was first published as a broadside for the National Poetry Festival (Allendale, Michigan) by the East Lansing Arts Workship Press, 1973. "How I analyze the Ideogram" and "I've always said that Gertrude Stein and Wittgenstein" were first published in *Sitting Frog: Poetry of the Naropa Institute* (edited by Rachel Peters and Eero Ruutilla), 1975.

Library of Congress Cataloging-in-Publication Data
Meltzer, David.
Two-way mirror : a poetry notebook / David Meltzer.
    pages cm
ISBN 978-0-87286-650-8 (hardback)
1. Poetics. 2. Poetry—Authorship. I. Title.
PS3563.E45T9 2015
808.1—dc23

                    2014048674

City Lights Books are published at the City Lights Bookstore
261 Columbus Avenue, San Francisco, CA 94133
www.citylights.com

*For Robert and Dorothy Hawley
of Berkeley's Oyez Press
& for my wife & heart's companion, Julie Rogers,
whose inspiration moved
this edition into being*

# TWO-WAY MIRROR

1977. I was 40 years old and typing on a geriatric Royal portable typewriter. I had long ago abandoned attempting the History of Everything. It was all around me and my limited (and limiting) focus couldn't see or sense it all despite my ego's chutzpah. Paying attention, focus, essential requisites for all writing were unfocused. Our stardom as folk rockers (Serpent Power, Tina and David) was minor and momentary. We were raising three young daughters and odd jobbing to keep it together.

Robert and Dorothy Hawley's Oyez Press had already published a couple of my books of poetry. Bob worked in the Rare Book/Western Americana room on the third floor of Oakland's long-gone Holmes Book Company. It was always a treat for me to go there and, in the late afternoon, drink shots of Jack Daniels, towered over by shelves of books. The wonderful polymath Alastair Johnson of Poltroon Press wrote a bibliographic accounting of the press. It's sadly out of print. Oyez published an eclectic collection of poets including William Everson/Brother Antoninus, Robert Duncan, Tom Parkinson, Janine Canan, Samuel Charters, and others during their run. The Hawleys were part of the last days of Black Mountain College and somehow happily wound up in El Cerrito, California. Besides having a deep expertise in Western Americana, Bob was a great listener to early jazz, which was invariably on the record player. Dorothy was a gifted and creative bookbinder. They both were remarkably generous to us and I feel immensely grateful to them for that.

I can't say exactly when the idea for *Two-Way Mirror*

came from, but when I told Bob about my plan to write a poetry primer, he agreed to take it on as an Oyez title. Maybe at every stage of age I thought I knew it all, or at least enough to taste it, and felt I could do something that wasn't brain-glue like so many textbooks I fled from.

Maybe it was my experience researching material for *Birth*, a mass-market anthology of historical and contemporary approaches to birth and birthing, that gave me a sense of context and interconnectedness. Every Saturday I'd go to the Doe Library on the UC Berkeley campus. It was eight floors of stacks reachable either by elevator or, my preference, iron circular staircases. Aisles of books on metal shelves. I'd browse in continual discovery. On a bottom shelf on one floor, huge vellum tomes in Latin with engravings of fetuses and wombs. On another floor the fat, green gold-stamped annuals and monographs of the American Ethnological Society, started in the 19th century. So much material on Native American ritual, lore, chant, on every facet of a tribe's social and cultural reality.

Sometime in this mix I began teaching in the Graduate Poetics program at New College of California. It was my first full-time teaching job, after teaching at a California prison and a private high school. This blessing came from its cofounder Duncan McNaughton. It was a unique program carried out by poets: Robert Duncan, Diane di Prima, Louis Patler, lasting five years before disbanding and transforming into an MFA program. It was an extraordinary five years. One of these days, some enterprising scholar would/should write a history of the Poetics Program. Its intent was not to replicate other writing programs, but instead to study the lineage and process of the poetic traditions informing us. It was to concentrate on the roots and routes of making poems. Many taught there: Robert Creeley, Anne Waldman, Gregory Corso, Leslie Scalapino, Judy Grahn, Susan Howe, Lorenzo Thomas, Gloria Frym, Lyn Hejinian, Michael Palmer, Michael McClure, Joanne Kyger, Tisa Walden, Jerome Rothenberg, Philip Whalen, Eileen Myles, Tom Raworth, Sharon Doubiago, Neeli Cherkovski, Jack Hirschman, and others whose names I'm embarrassed to blank on.

This experience was central to my thinking and acting on the poem, exposing me to shifting concepts of theory, philosophy, the social sciences, history, spirituality. Much of the additional writing in this book comes out of notes and talks given to classes at New College. It's odd to note a difficulty with language and meaning around the edges. I'm reminded of Wittgenstein's ongoing frustration with the word "red."

•

In the original edition of *Two-Way Mirror* was an insert to be sent to assorted educational facilities. Some of it read as follows:

> TWO-WAY MIRROR can be read by anyone who wishes to, but it is primarily a book of texts intended for people who might be interested in reading and/or writing poetry. It's meant for the beginner and functions as a book of basics arranged in such a way as to challenge and provoke the novice.
>
> Much of the book's parts have been effectively used in poetry workshops that I've conducted in high schools, both public and private, in California. Much of my concern has been to reach and activate the capacity for poetry and poem-making latent but approachable in many young people. Being able to personalize language, to express one's self out of the group-context, is a useful and ex-

pansive tool. Being made to understand the power and magic of language helps them to derive greater pleasure from literature (and music) and serves to expand wider cultural awareness.

The book can be looked at as a primer, an approach to the creative principle embodied in poetry—approaching an art too often shrouded by inadequate cultural and educational concepts. I've witnessed the great satisfaction that creation brings to the beginner and have been shocked to learn how fear of poetry and/or art stems from poor educational preparation. Poetry, art, music, should be broadly taught in schools starting from Kindergarten and on. More importantly, teachers should be well-instructed in these areas by diverse creative artists as to the mysteries of their art and craft.

It's hoped that both student and teacher will be able to find some use for this book. Or find some fault to argue with. Get mad at it or me or both or none. But by all means respond and engage with its material and find out what works for you or for your students.

•

Now, almost 40 years later, what's changed? In the '70s to '90s, there was the Poetry in the Schools movement, which started in New York and migrated spottily across the country and landed in California, only to be gradually underfunded in our time, along with other arts programs. In colleges and universities, poetry instruction and production were rationalized and professionalized. Poetry publishing remains and retains a loss-leader role. Small adventurous presses and journals persist in the margins and, of course, the Internet has further fragmented poetry online. Book publishing & bookstores are caving in, producing less and less and worrying more and more about their commercial viability.

In the decades following the publication of this book, much has happened to destabilize earlier assumptions. Poetic movements, as they should, have challenged whatever is the dominant canon and cant. Unknown poets have been retrieved and reclaimed. The profound social impact of the '60s allowed for challenging interventions of race, sexuality, ethnicity, a radical shift that became absorbed into the higher educational bureaucracies. As with too many resistance movements, it became embraced and neutralized. No U.S. poet that I know of has ever been executed by the state, whereas over the world too many have been imprisoned and murdered for their work and its impact on their people.

Today the Doe Library has been retrofitted. No more eight floors of stacks, instead a subterranean descent of floors with books in rolling bookcases you pull out with something like a mariner's wheel. The major part of floor spaces is now devoted to tables and outlets for computer use. The ascent of the computer and the descent of the book are ongoing and, like so many technologies, have become naturalized, environments one lives in with less and less question or reflection. (It is no wonder there are so many new gizmos prefaced by "i".)

But there's been a valuable counter-movement to before the book, the page, a return to orality via rap, slams, performance poetry. Despite its fragmentation, the need and desire for writing, hearing, reading poetry insists itself to be. Like most creative gestures, it's a sign of both acceptance and resistance.

•

# First Lesson

1. This is a man.


2. This is a woman.

3. That is a woman.


4. That is a man.

---

NEW WORDS: this is a man that woman

---

This is a book of basics. Like an almanac. Variables. All over the place. No sure thing.

First steps on reading and writing poems. It's a fantasy. You've already begun.

Map of my effort to assemble a book. Yo-yo. Topographic spread of a treasure hunt. A book inside a book and often no book at all. Shrapnel. Corkscrew through history. Like history it is chaos. You finally have to write your own book.

A poem is perhaps the highest form of verbal communication.

It illuminates and it conceals.

It is as precise and as vague as a mirror.

This book starts and ends at the beginning. Voices come at you from all sides. Gullible sparks flourish. Good luck.

# PART ONE

*Let us have friends here!*
*It is time to know our faces.*
*Only with flowers*
*can our songs enrapture.*
*We will have gone to His house,*
*but our word*
*shall live here on earth.*
*We will go, leaving behind*
*our grief, our song.*
*For this will be known,*
*the song shall remain real.*
*We will have gone to His house,*
*but our word*
*shall live here on earth.*

Pre-Columbian Mexico

I saw a fishpond all on fire
I saw a house bow to a squire
I saw a parson twelve feet high
I saw a cottage near the sky
I saw a balloon made of lead
I saw a coffin drop down dead
I saw two sparrows run a race
I saw two horses making lace
I saw a girl just like a cat
I saw a kitten wear a hat
I saw a man who saw these too
And said though strange they all were true.

•

The poet asks his seven-year-old daughter, What is a poem?
Why is it different than just talking?
She answers, I don't know. No, I can't figure it out.
It's shorter.
It's shorter and it rhymes.
It makes more sense than a book.
It's sweeter.
It's nice.

•

The poem happens on a moment-to-moment basis.

One minute it is all there. Clear as a bell. Resounding. The next moment the magic leaves the words and what is on the page becomes nothing more than dull black marks as mediocre as yesterday's newspaper.

•

But more importantly:

Is the poem on the page the poem within you?

•

Poetry is speech that attempts to be song.

It's a way of rising above speech to create an alternative language whose parts are closer to music. Whose parts are closer to the heart. Whose parts close in on the mind. Whose parts converge and become one.

Poetry is musical speech.

•

Poetry's a magic act.

•

An instinctive rhythm is rooted in the heart of nature: breathing, walking, the act of procreation and the heartbeat. It has also been suggested that the repeated syllables of infant babble talk are to some extent influenced by the rhythmic sounds of the heart first heard by the infant in the mother's womb. The rhythmic sounds of nature are impressive and mysterious and they belong to a different order of sound from the warbling of birds and the chattering of monkeys. For earliest man rhythmic sound was a magic tool in his struggle to understand and control nature when art, the pursuit of beauty, was a luxury he could not afford.

—Leonard Williams

•

Breath. Voice. To sound. To make a sound. To take sound from breath through throat, palate, tongue against teeth against mouth cave. To utter a name.

To name.

Tree. Bird. Sky. Earth. You.

The woman begins to comprehend your naming and like an echo repeats the sound back to you.

Tree. Bird. Sky. Earth. You.

The man and woman chant it. Their sound runs together into a river of tones. They delight in the music of naming. Treebirdskyearthyou. All that there is, all that is known. What a wonder! Tree. Bird. Sky. Earth. You.

•

. . . And thereafter I saw the darkness changing into a watery substance, which was unspeakabley tossed about, and gave forth smoke as from fire; and I heard it making an indescribable sound of lamentation; for there was sent forth from it an inarticulate cry. But from the Light there came forth a holy Word (or "Speech"), which took its stand upon the watery substance; and methought this Word was the voice of the Light.

And Poimandres spoke for me to hear, and said to me, "Do you understand the meaning of what you have seen?" "Tell me its meaning," I said, "and I shall know." "That Light," he said, "is I, even Mind, the first God, who was before the watery substance which appeared out of darkness; and the Word which came forth from the Light is son of God." "How so?" said I. "Learn my meaning," said he, "by looking at what you yourself have in you; for in you too, the word is son, and the mind is father of the word. They are not separate one from the other; for life is the union of word and mind." Said I, "For this I thank you."

"Now fix your thought upon the Light," he said, "and learn to know it." And when he had thus spoken, he gazed long upon me, eye to eye, so that I trembled at his aspect. And when I raised my head again, I saw in my mind that the Light consisted of innumerable Powers, and had come to be an ordered world, but a world without bounds ("intelligible world" as opposed to the "sensible world"). This I perceived in thought, seeing it by reason of the word which Poimandres had spoken to me. And when I was amazed, he spoke again, and said to me, "You have seen in your mind the archetypal form, which is prior to the beginning of things, and is limitless." Thus Poimandres spoke to me.

—*Corpus Hermeticum*

•

To place himself. To end exile. To replace himself. Naming. Tombstones. Magic.

The beginning of words and names marks the beginning of exile. Being apart from what's in front of my nose.

In the beginning was the end. In the beginning was the word.

In many of the world's sacred books the earth, the universe, man, animals, the whole circus, is created by a word.

Magical nouns.

Seeds.

•

Songs are thoughts, sung with the breath when people are moved by great forces and ordinary speech no longer suffices. Man is moved just like the ice-floe sailing here and there out in the current. His thoughts are driven by a flowing force when he feels joy, when he feels fear, when he feels sorrow. Thoughts can wash over him like a flood, making his breath come in gasps and his heart throb. Something like an abatement in the weather will keep him thawed up. And then it will happen that we, who always think we are small, will feel still smaller. And we will fear to use words. But it will happen that the words we need will come of themselves. When the words we want to use shoot up of themselves—we get a new song.

—Orpingalik

•

Therefore Ogotommêli says, "The word is for all in this world; it must be exchanged, so that it goes and comes, for it is good to give and to receive the forces of life."

—Marcel Griaule

•

### The Train

1. This is a train.
2. A man and a woman are on the train.
3. The man's bag is on that seat.
4. His coat and shirts are in his bag.
5. The woman's box is on a seat.
6. Her hat is in the box.
7. A bag is in her hand.

---

NEW WORDS: train on seat gets from

---

If there were no word, all forces would be frozen, there would be no procreation, no change, no life. "There is nothing that there is not; whatever we have a name for, that is," so speaks the wisdom of the Yoruba priests. The proverb signifies that the naming, the enunciation, produces what it names. Naming is an incantation, a creative act. What we cannot conceive of is unreal; it does not exist. But every human thought, once expressed, becomes reality. For the word holds the course of things in train and changes and transforms them. And since the word has this power, every word is an effective word, every word is binding. There is no "harmless," noncommittal word. Every word has consequences. Therefore the word binds the *muntu*.[1] And the *muntu* is responsible for his word.

—Janheinz Jahn

•

---

1. A Bantu word usually translated as "man" . . . But the concept of *muntu* embraces living and dead, ancestors and deified ancestors: gods. The unity expressed by the inclusive concept of *muntu* is one of the characteristics of African culture.

The need for speech is one matter, the need for song another.

When the basic words are there then song begins. It is basic words which paradoxically set out to transcend language. It is language used to reach a place beyond language. Language is the rope the Indian uses in his trick.

Language as ritual used to add to or magnify everyday reality. As a bridge toward the gods who were, in the beginning, angry and whimsical and in constant need of song and chant. By imitating nature song attempted to borrow some of nature's magic. The god or gods were then, as always, nature.

•

Sometimes I think I understand it all. But when I try to put the secret into words there is no secret. My words look curiously foolish on the page, useless.

•

In the process of inventing civilization there grew a need to make words more permanent. To transfer them to substances more durable than a moment and, as usual, compete with what man thought his god and gods were doing in their heavens and hells.

Imagination took words from the air and carved them into stone, etched them into bark, penned them onto parchment. Words from newly minted alphabets placed onto any form that could bear the imprint.

Trap words from the air. Contain them.

Alphabets are the language of time. The page is a strange zoo.

•

This paradox remains even in elements of our own disastrously advanced culture: despite the invention, realization and often dominating influence of letters speaking through time, many still insist that a spoken word from a master to a disciple conveys more mystery and truth than a van-load of wisdom books.

•

We are dealing with the invention of letters placed on a page. The page is the space where the poetry of our time takes place.

•

Writing begins with the abbreviation of what's actual. A rendering of the real world into a picture-code.

Professor David Diringer—distinguished authority in the history of alphabets and the development of writing—explains the process of alphabet-genesis in five rungs.

1) Picture-writing or pictography. The most primitive form of true writing. A picture represents the thing shown. Sun drawn as sun, man as man, dog as dog, etc. You can see how easy it is to record straight narrative in pictographs. Twentieth-century colleagues and tribesmen have comic books, non-verbal signs. It's a writing you watch but it has no words. No voice.

2) Ideographic writing, much more sophisticated. The pictograph represents not so much the thing shown but instead deals with an underlying idea associated with those things. A circle might not only be the sun but might be the moon or a time of day or "day." The pictures become symbols and take on more complicated meanings. They are not necessarily what they seem to be.

3) Transitional scripts. Transition from symbol into a more abstract form. Also a combination of pictograph and ideograph and partly phonetic symbols arranged in various ways. A process developing toward the alphabet. A refining process. An abstracting process.

4) Phonetic writing. In picture-writing and the pure ideographic scripts, there is no connection between what's depicted and the name for it. The symbols can be "read" in any language. Phonetic writing becomes the graphic counterpart of recording speech. Each element in this writing system corresponds to a specific sound in the language represented. The signs no longer represent objects or ideas but, instead, represent sounds or groups of sounds.

The symbols, being no longer self-interpreting pictures, must be explained through the language they represent. The single signs may be of any shape, and generally there is no connection between the external form of the symbol and the sound it represents. Phonetic writing may be syllabic or alphabetic, the former being the less advanced of the two. (Diringer)

5) Syllabic writing. Where single symbols represent syllables or vowels so that a group of syllables conveys a spoken word.

Which leads to the development of alphabet. End of the line. The highly developed fast-food system. Convenient, easily adaptable. Thanks to the simplicity and adaptability of alphabet, writing has become very common. No longer the exclusive realm of the priests and other privileged classes.

•

What is the virtue of letters?

They are mute organs that speak—a body without a soul, and without life, guiding thought—dead ones, knowing more than the living—a hand speaking better than the tongue—an eye hearing better than the ear, without either noise or sound—speech without a tongue—hearing without an ear—language without words—forms of voice—a messenger uttering the truth without knowing it—the dead teaching the living—memory with no one guiding it—the understanding of the dead—the principal skill of the art of the living—the preservation of all arts and sciences—and the demonstration of all that is demonstrable.

—From *Barddas*

•

In African poetry . . . the expression is always in the service of the content; it is never a question of expressing *oneself*, but of expressing *something*, and, indeed, with a view to the results, for African poetry exists as *function*. Nor is the African poet ever concerned with his inner nature, with *his* individuality.

Here lies the essential differences between African and modern European poetry in general. Benn writes: "The expressionistic poet is expressing nothing different from poets of times and schools: *his* relation to nature, his love, his sorrow, his thoughts about God." This is indeed true to a great extent for western poetry from Sappho to Benn. But for African poetry it is not true at all. The African poet does not express *his* relation to nature, but places "Nature" (*Kintu*) at his service, rouses it into life, steers and manipulates it. In the love poem he does not express *his* love, but love as such, a force in which he shares. The love poem is more than conversation, courtship, play: it is Nommo, word seed in the most concrete sense. "When one speaks to a woman, one makes her fertile," writes Ogotommêli. "Or at least one introduces into her a celestial seed, one puts her in condition to be humanly fertilized." In the same way the poet expresses sorrow as such, and expresses not his own, but *the* "thoughts" about God. "For in the last analysis every artistic manifestation is collective, created for all and shared by all," writes Senghor. "Because they are functional and collective, Negro-African literature and art are committed. They commit the person, and not merely the individual."

The European poet is an individual and expresses what *he* feels, thinks, has experienced, wants. The African poet is a person, and that means sorcerer, prophet, teacher. He expresses what *must be*. His "I" is not therefore "collective" in the European sense; it is not non-individual. He speaks *to* the community and *for* them. He has a social task which raises him above the community: the most important poets, Césaire, Senghor, Rabémananjara, Guillén, Ortiz and many others are politicians who exercise an official function. Their functional character does not prevent them from saying "I," but this "I" is always a "we," and every I-statement includes a binding imperative.

From this it follows that African poetry, old and new, is determined by responsibility. Poetry does not describe, but arranges series of images which alter reality in the direction of the future, which create, produce, invoke, and bring about the future. The present interpreted by the poetry is subordinate to the future. African poets take no delight in drawing the present for its own sake or for the pleasure of the drawing. The present is material for transformation; it is Kintu. It is dissolved into particular images, which the poet arranges anew according to their power as examples, sometimes to terrify, sometimes to attract. He counts up what he holds to be true and what false, and groups it, not according to a system inherent in the things, but according to the force inherent in the images themselves. This does not exclude a rational context; on the contrary, since all the images are related to a purpose, each one has its meaningful relation to it. But reason is—as in all poetry—the slave of expression. The poem is meant to convince not through logic but through fascination.

—Janheinz Jahn

•

A poet is a man who dreams wide-awake; but he can guide his dreams or imaginings to symmetrical form, and to a logical conclusion or coherence. With the painter and sculptor it is the same. When the *alter-ego* works harmoniously with the *waking will,* we call it Imagination.

But when the *alter-ego* draws decidedly on latent forces, or powers unknown to the waking Me, I am amazed. He does it often enough, *that* is certain. Then we have Mystery. And it is out of this that men have drawn the conclusion that they have two or three souls—an astral spirit, a power of prophecy, the art of leaving the body, and the entire machinery of occultism . . . it steals into our waking life in many ways. It comes in emotions, presentiments, harp tones, mystical conceptions, and mingling of images or ideas, and incomprehensible deductions, which are sometimes, of course, prophetic. It has nothing in common with common sense; therefore it is to some un-common sense, or to others non-sense. Sometimes it *is* one or the other. Agreeable sensations and their harmony become the Beautiful. These blend and produce a general aesthetic sense. It becomes mystical, and is easily worked on by the *alter-ego.* The most inspired passages of every poet on the beauty of Nature betray clearly the influence and hidden power of the Dream in waking life.

—Charles Godfrey Leland

•

The greatest poet hardly knows pettiness or triviality. If he breathes into anything that was before thought small it dilates with the grandeur and life of the universe. He is a seer . . . he is individual . . . he is complete in himself . . . the others are as good as he, only he sees it and they do not. He is not one of the chorus . . . he does not stop for any regulations . . . he is president of regulation. What the eyesight does to the rest he does to the rest. Who knows what curious mystery of eyesight? The other senses corroborate themselves, but this is removed from any proof but its own and foreruns the identities of the spiritual world. A single glance of it mocks all the investigations of man and the instruments and books of the earth and all reasoning. What is marvellous? what is unlikely? what is impossible or baseless or vague? after you have once just opened the space of a peach-pit and given audience to far and near and to the sunset and had all things enter with electric swiftness softly and duly without confusion or jostling or jam.

—Walt Whitman

•

*Muses.* In Greek mythology originally the Nymphs of inspiring springs, then goddesses of song in general, afterwards the representatives of the various kinds of poetry, arts and sciences. In Homer, who now speaks of one, and now of many Muses, but without specifying their number or their names, they are considered as goddesses dwelling in Olympus, who at meals of the gods sing sweetly to the lyre of Apollo, inspire the poet and prompt his song. Hesiod *(Theogony* 52—, 76—,) calls them the nine daughters of Zeus and Mnemosyne, born in Pieria, and mentions their names, to which we shall at the same time add the province and the attributes afterwards assigned to each. (1) CALLIOPE (she of the fair voice), in Hesiod the noblest of all, the Muse of *epic song*; among her attributes are a wax tablet and a pencil. (2) CLIO (she that extols), the Muse of *history*; with a scroll. (3) EUTERPE (she that gladdens), the Muse of *lyric song*; with the double flute. (4) THALIA (she that flourishes), the Muse of *comedy* and bucolic poetry; with the comic mask, the ivy wreath, and the shepherd's staff. (5) MELPOMENE (she that sings), the Muse of *tragedy*; with tragic mask, ivy wreath, and occasionally with attributes of individual heroes, *e.g.* the club, the sword. (6) TERPSICHORE (she that rejoices in the dance), the Muse of *dancing*; with the lyre. (7) ERATO (the lovely one), the Muse of *erotic poetry*; with a smaller lyre. (8) POLYMNIA or POLYHYMNIA (she that is rich in hymns), the Muse of serious *sacred songs*; usually represented as veiled and pensive. (9) URANIA (the heavenly), the Muse of *astronomy*; with the celestial globe.

Three older Muses were sometimes distinguished from these. MELETE (Meditation), MNEME (Remembrance), AOIDE (Song), whose worship was said to have been introduced by the Aloidae, Otus, and Ephialtes, near Mount Helicon. Thracian settlers in the Pierian district at the foot of Olympus and of Helicon in Boeotia are usually mentioned as the original founders of this worship. At both these places were their oldest sanctuaries. According to the general belief, the favourite haunts of the Muses were certain springs, near which temples and statues had been erected in their honour: Castalia, at the foot of Mount Parnassus, and Aganippe and Hippocrene, on Helicon, near the towns of Ascra and Thespiae. After the decline of Ascra, the inhabitants of Thespiae attended to the worship of the Muses and to the arrangements for the musical contests in their honour that took place once in five years. They were also adored in many other places in Greece. Thus the Athenians offered them sacrifices in the schools, while the Spartans did so before battle. As the inspiring Nymphs of the springs they were early connected with Dionysus; the god of the poets, Apollo, is looked upon as their leader (*Musagetes*), with whom they share the knowledge of past, present, and future. As beings that gladden men and gods with their song, they are described by Hesiod as dwelling on Olympus along with the Charites and Himeros. They were represented in art as virgin goddesses with long garments of many folds, and frequently with a cloak besides; they were not distinguished by special attributes until comparatively later times. The Roman poets identified them with the Italian *Camenae,* prophetic Nymphs of springs and goddesses of birth, who had a grove at Rome outside the *Porta Capena.* The Greeks gave the title of Muses to their nine most distinguished poetesses: Praxilla, Moero, Anyte, Erinna, Telesilla, Corinna, Nossis, Myrtis, and Sappho.

—*Dictionary of Classical Antiquities* Oskar Seffert

•

We are led to believe in a lie
When we see *with* not *through* the eye.

—William Blake

•

We do not hate the human beings that listen to it, read it, make comments on it. They are like you. It is as if they or you observed one continual movement of surf breaking against the rocks. A textbook of poetry is created to explain. We do not hate the human beings that listen to it, the moment of the surf breaking.

It is fake. The real poetry is beyond us, beyond them, breaking like glue. And the rocks were not there and the real birds, they seemed like seagulls, were nesting on the real rocks. Close to the edge. The ocean (the habit of seeing) Christ, the Logos unbelieved in, where the real edge of it is.

A private language. Carried about us, them. Ununderstanding.

—Jack Spicer

•

I have no space, no time. I exist as you, only you, you within me. I am not a madman. Not even artist, nor shaman. I am the sun, this moment, total of the visions inherent and inseparable in us all, transmitted through me. My fiber. Your spine. Our Chakra. Xylophone vertebrae. Han Shan dancing the ghostdance. Everything a change, alternative, excitement. It is wrapped around us all. And the gypsy, the hidden dreamer dreaming us, swings on through it, penetrates, leads to the center. Pops the bubble.

•

No message is contained in this act. There is only rejoicing. The word, the voice, is not very powerful. It goes back to the mouths of ourselves that speak it. Therein lies the power.

—John Brandi

•

Another important point. Having located your local poet, take the time to read his work before knocking on his door with your poems.

•

# PART TWO

*Three things which a Bard ought to do:*
*to listen; to look; and keep secret.*
*To listen; to expect; and to be silent.*

—From *Barddas*.

I'd like to tell you how I started writing and why I prefer poetry to prose and why I chose poetry as my art and discipline.

The first poem came through me when I was eleven years old.

Some moments you do not forget.

If there had been a clock in my room—it was early afternoon—I could also give you the exact clock-time that the first poem came through me and went into my fingers onto the keyboard of my first typewriter to emerge crazily onto a piece of Woolworth Herald Square typing paper.

Up to that moment I filled notebooks and pads and scraps of usable paper with adventures, curious drawings, diaries, futurisms, philosophy, and fanciful tales. Before the poem entered the picture I was hard at work on my most ambitious project to date: a four-volume History of Everything—from the Beginning to the dawn of what was to be known as the Atomic Age. It was handwritten in pencil in four Square Deal Composition notebooks with black-and-white speckled cardboard covers that held at least 200 blue-lined pages per volume.

I don't know exactly why I wanted to write the History of Everything, but I felt a need to at least express the questions (mysteries) that I couldn't find answers or words for. I thought that if I started at the Beginning and wrote my way to Now I would get, in the process, at least some of the answers to the mysteries. But even the Beginning was a mystery to me. I startled my mother when I told her I could remember what it looked like inside her womb.

—Oh, you and your imagination! she said and went back to basting the roast.

I asked my father to tell me how it all began.

—How what began?

—Everything. The world, man, all of it, from the beginning.

—Are you kidding? he asked.

—No, I'm really serious.

We were walking home from the candystore, which meant three blocks of continual questions I kept asking my father.

He tried answering them, but whenever he started to answer one question I'd have to ask him another.

A week later he took me to a secondhand bookstore on Fourth Avenue in Manhattan and bought me a copy of *The Outline of History* by H.G. Wells and a copy of *The Story of Mankind* by Hendrick Van Loon.

When I got home I read the Contents page of the Wells book and felt large with learning. Van Loon's illustrations in his history convinced me that I should illustrate my own history.

I set to work with these two books, supplementing them with pre-horror E.C. Comics also dealing with the history of mankind. After a couple of weeks of writing my hand got stiff and my father donated his old portable typewriter to the cause. It was a Hermes Rocket made in Switzerland and was small enough to fit on my lap. I took a few days off from the project to learn how to use the typewriter. It took longer than I thought; in fact, I still don't know how to use a typewriter the right way. But that's another story.

I did learn the magic of a typewriter. It was like printing your own book. Wanting to earn my living as a professional writer, I began typing out the first issue of a neighborhood newspaper. My plan was to carbon copy each page and sell it to the neighbors. But I got bogged down in the mechanics of trying to type out a newspaper on folded pieces of typing paper swollen with carbon paper. Justified margins proved to be the final mind-boggle. It was back to the History.

•

At eleven years of age I knew as much about poetry as I did about Everything and typing, which was next to nothing. Poetry was a shape on the page that did not fill the page out like prose did. Actually I don't think I had ever read any poetry. None of my books had poems in them except for a leather-bound anthology called *Magic Casements.* I looked through the book, enjoyed its thin pages and wobbly flexible binding, but the poems inside it were as remote as calculus or nuclear physics.

Yet I was beginning to feel that prose was a commonplace form of communication and that there must be a form beyond prose to express what I wanted to say.

What a drudgery it had become to write sentence after sentence leading into paragraphs that after a while become chapters and finally that's over and you have to type out an Index and a Bibliography. All of those words and sentences and paragraphs and footnotes to tell the History of Everything and all the time knowing next to nothing. The more I wrote the less I knew, the more dissatisfied I became. I had this strong feeling to express something inside that had no face and seemed to defy language.

•

It was the time of Manhattan's bicentennial. Public schools were invited to compete in art and writing contests to celebrate the event.

I was in the sixth grade and Mrs. Callahan was our teacher. She told me to write a poem honoring Manhattan, since I was good at writing and last year wrote a tribute to Mayor LaGuardia who had died. (The piece appeared in the P.S. 232 newspaper and marked my first appearance in print.)

—I don't know how to write poems, I told Mrs. Callahan (which meant I didn't know anything about rhyming or meter or verse forms).

Mrs. Callahan told me not to worry. She said I should concentrate on defining a feeling or feelings I had about the city and make it into a poem.

Carole Grossman sat across the aisle and looked at me in a way that said you had better try making that poem because if you don't you will never be welcome into my living room again. In her living room we would help each other with homework and sometimes recite dramatic passages out of Shakespeare. Often she would go to the upright piano, sit on the round stool before the keyboard, and play *Malagueña*—which she knew was a particular favorite of mine. It amazed me every time Carole Grossman opened a book of music, spread the pages flat against the piano and played.

—Sure, I told Mrs. Callahan. —I'll write a poem.

—It can be in free verse, added Mrs. Callahan. —It doesn't have to rhyme.

God bless Mrs. Callahan.

Not wanting to prolong the moment, I did not ask Mrs. Callahan what "free verse" was. I nodded knowingly. Smart ass. And that was that.

•

After supper I asked my father what free verse was.

He thought a bit and said it probably was poetry that didn't rhyme.

—Is that all?

—Well, I'm not sure. I know it doesn't rhyme and that each poem develops its own particular rhythms, and a free verse poem seems to use a variety of line lengths. . . .

He took out the *Magic Casements* anthology and showed me a poem by Amy Lowell called *Patterns* and I remember only the last line of it: *Christ! why must patterns be?*

—That's free verse, said my father. —Why don't you read more free verse poems so you can get a better idea of what it's all about.

—I don't have time, I said.

I should have said, to be honest, that I wasn't interested in anyone else's work except my own.

I decided to invent poetry for myself and it would be in my own voice and rhythms. Just like that.

•

The first poem that came through me was about the subway system.

I say that the poem "came through me" because I had no clear idea of what I wanted to say or how I was going to say it. Everything happened suddenly.

I just started writing the poem and automatically began to think in a different way about words, repetitions, meanings, the sound of language.

It rushed out faster than my typing ability could deal with, but I continued, figuring that I'd be able to unscramble it all when it was over.

The subway surged and flowed through underground

tunnels beneath a city whose buildings soar to the sky. The subway cars moving through arterial passageways carrying "the life's blood of the city / the people."

It was as if I was singing and speaking and acting all at once. An inner voice took over and snipped off lines where it felt they ended, extending lines where it felt the voice needed room for full-scale chanting.

Another compartment of my self was aware that the poem wanted to make the subway both real and metaphor. Right then I realized that a poem should always deal with actual things if it wanted to suggest forms beyond the actual.

That confounded History of Everything set me up for this revelation. By writing a poem on the Manhattan subway system I learned that Everything wasn't enough. I learned that Everything was too much and therefore beyond me.

One thing at a time. The poem taught me that.

I saw how word leads to word and how each step is its own adventure. Each touching-down as monumental as stepping into the moon's dust.

The poem is always going somewhere and the poet is in charge of seeing that it gets there.

It dawned on me that Everything was held in any-thing—any thing or person. The art and magic was the ability to describe a thing in clear language. To arrange the telling in such a way as to make that thing an object of great beauty or mystery, and to try to make that thing or person appear on the page as a presence, essential and defined. To give it a dimension unnoticed before the poet's intervention. A jar in Tennessee or a fishing boat in Gloucester or a blade of grass or a red wheelbarrow.

My poem on the subway system went on for 10 pages and I described the whole process as best as I could. It included a loud hymn to the rush-hour crush and ended with a new day slowly and dramatically dawning.

When I was finished, I knew I was finished. I sat back in amazement at what I had done.

•

# PART THREE

*The Doctor say to pay as you earn*
*The Sparrow say we paying to learn*
*But me father say he selling the ax*
*For when the collector come to pay off the income tax*

—The Mighty Sparrow

History is being there when you are also here.

History is being here, not there.

History is nowhere. It's an invention. Its nervous system is compiled out of poetry.

One way or another, we make our marks against time.

Scratch scratch scratch

•

A fast pre-history of the English poem.

It was both news and song. It existed in the air and was carried from place to place by people who had a knack for the job.

To begin with, the poem was a song informing people of the news outside their village. It was sung data.

And it was sung because songs are easier to memorize and easier to pass on to others. The poem was history set to music, a one-man opera.

•

3 things which a Bard ought to do:
listen carefully to every thing
look fully at every thing
and hold his peace soundly
unless there be sound reason for his speech.

—From *Barddas*

•

The radical difference between the musical custom of the Indian and our own race is that, originally, the Indians used song as a means of accomplishing definite results. Singing was not a trivial matter, like the flute-playing of the young men. It was used in treating the sick, in securing success in war and the hunt, and in every undertaking which the Indian felt was beyond his power as an individual. An Indian said, "If a man is to do something more than human he must have more than human power."

—Frances Densmore

•

*Angel of Song*—Radueriel (Vretil), who is also the choir-master of the muses. In Koranic lore, the angel of song is Israfel or Uriel. In rabbinic lore, the angel is Shemiel (Shemeal, Shammiel) or Metatron. The last named is called "Master of Heavenly Song."

—*A Dictionary of Angels*

•

Song begins when you discover song. When song reaches you. Rockabye Baby. Even before that. When there are no words. Just the drum of mother's heart comforting you as you sleep and sail within her center.

Song begins when you sing a song after hearing a song sung to you. When you repeat the tones and order the music. It begins when you have no words.

Everything that comes out of your sparkling baby mouth are sounds which are songs which soon enough become words which become sentences which are shaped into paragraphs and into contracts and newspaper headlines and all of it takes the voice farther and farther away from song.

Song begins and ends with you. Like the pieces of sound they are made of, songs are something you either pass on as the mystery of history or they become sounds you pass on. No thanks.

Which is a chilling paragraph for which I hand you a sack of rock salt. Do you remember the first song you ever heard? the first song you ever made? It's there, locked up with all the other beginnings. Like Rosebud stuck in the chaos of accumulation, the debris of self.

•

"How can I know if I write verse or prose," Reb Elati remarked. "I am rhythm."

And elsewhere: "Without rhythm, you would not see the sun every morning.

"You could not.

"Rhythm is internal. It is the rhythm of fate.

"No matter how you tried, you could neither go faster nor move more slowly.

"You could not but move in harmony with your blood, with your mind, with your heart.

"In harmony.

"You could not be fast or slow.

"You could not.

"Is it conceivable for the moon to come after the moon?

"I went to God, because God was my fate.

"I went to the word of God, because the word of God was my fate.

"I went to the word.

"To make it my gesture.

"I went.

"And I am going."

—Edmond Jabès

•

## 1.

A singer performs words.

So does a poet.

But there's a big difference between the poem on the page and the poem in the air.

What is it?

## 2.

The poem performs on the page.

The page is the space a poem lives within.

Air is the space a song lives within.

A poem is not a song.

A poem is not a song even though it has its own music and rhythm and can, if you care to do it, be set to music and then sung like a song.

A poem written on the page is not a song. A song is a lyric on a piece of music-paper that is meant to be sung.

A poem is on the page, not in the air.

An artist who paints pictures is not a movie director.

A painter is not a photographer.

A poet writes poems.

Poetry is not television.

A song-writer writes lyrics for music.

## 3.

Bob Dylan, Cole Porter, Chuck Berry, Noel Coward, Randy Newman, Lorenz Hart, Hank Williams, Ira Gershwin, etc., are not poets even though they have written lyrics that come close.

### 4.

A poem is on the page. Its "sound" occurs within the silence you bring to it.

A poem is its own music.

It doesn't need engineers, producers, musicians, a vocal group, etc., to enhance its power or purpose.

The poem on the page is its own music. A complete creation.

### 5.

Great song-writers do not have to be compared to great poets. Great song-writers do not have to even be compared to each other. It is foolish to say that Robert Johnson wrote songs similar to the poems of John Donne.

Genre is the key and sets the limit and within each space is an infinite variety.

Listening to blues or Top Ten songs or C&W songs or *cante hondo* or rock and roll, etc., is invaluable basic training for poets. In fact, essential.

The language out of the specific realm is invariably charged with its special grace and invention. It does not want to be compared to anything else. Nor blessed or knighted by those who think Art is king and vox-pop the rabble.

•

Perhaps I had better begin by frankly admitting that when I was a younger man I used to harbor a secret feeling of commiseration for poets. To my mind poets were men who were trying to make music with nothing but words at their command. I suppose there exist at all times some few men who have that much magic in them, but words at best will always seem to a composer a poor substitute for tones—if you want to make music, that is. Later on, after I had some slight reading acquaintance with the poetry of Hart Crane and Gerard Manley Hopkins, I came gradually to see that music and poetry were perhaps closer kin than I had at first realized. I came gradually to see that beyond the music of both arts there is an essence that joins them—an area where meanings behind the notes and meanings beyond the words spring from some common source.

—Aaron Copland

•

Part of me sings with meadowlark and loon.
The other part squawks with crows.

•

When I solo, I listen to the piano and the other instruments, and I try to play against what they're doing. But the ideal way to play would be to concentrate to such an extent that all you could hear was yourself, which is something I've been trying to do all my life, to make my music absolutely pure. You either hit home runs or you strike out in this business. Anything in between, you're second rate.

—Bobby Hackett

•

America's speech waterfalls forth in meltingpot tongues of Babel in telegraphic ads, pop songs, street-corner rapping, barroom bluster and brag, put-ons, bad-mouthing, put-downs;

the home-made bibles of Whitman, Melville or Andrew Jackson Davis, Thomas Lake Harris or L. Ron Hubbard;

the stream-clear prose of Thoreau or Hemingway or Gertrude Stein's devotionals;

the sportscaster's spiel tracing a horserace over the radio;

the hawking, squawking, conning and jiving, preaching and teaching, wheeling and dealing, jive-ass realms of speech;

the hard sell, the soft sell;

gossip columnists, breathless, telling-all;

rug-cutting, right on, telling It like It is, can you dig it?

letting it all hang out, hang in there, anyway, it's all se-mantic, outasight;

hermetical trade-lingo, jargon of short-order cooks, truckdrivers, piledrivers, jazz musicians, car mechanics, ste-reo buffs, tool talk, farm talk, technological speech forms machine-sprouted;

self-protective tribal languages, shields against outside and degrading power languages—

the black man's linguistic counterattack on white Amer-ica's word-gas clouds webbed with blood, the same cloud hanging over the American Indian, the Chicano, the Puerto Rican;

curt New England speech brittle as icicles;

the Southerner's smoothing-out drawls;

the Midwestern flat plain speech;

shtetl to ghetto Yiddishisms of Eastern cities;

shop-talk, cop-talk, bop-talk, TV hypno-verbs, phoney baloney, hot air;

these sounds, the languages, codes and messages, meet in the ears and eyes of poets who have been Jacob wrestling with Europe ever since landing on Plymouth Rock.

America was claimed: a new place, a new space to build great cities on.

The poets immediately and innocently and arrogantly began to fashion a language to meet and match America's impossible largeness.

•

There is no "mainstream" in American poetry. That concept is an invention much like American history. No matter how they teach literature in school, it isn't so. White pure orderly even perfect limited. Endless smile in a toothpaste ad.

Don't believe a word they or me or anybody else tells you. Unless it's in a language that makes absolute sense to you.

There is no American language, only a compost heap of all the other languages brought here. We're all from somewhere else and should never forget the music of the language of our forebears. Nor should we forget the the language of the streets. Combined they are the ladders of our art's ascent.

•

It's head work, brain work. (Philip Whalen called a book of his poetry *Brain Candy*.)

It's the mind pulling its muscles together, flexing its mountains.

It's the mind burrowing into itself.

It's the mind turning its pages.

•

Write what you want to read.

The more you write, the more you read, the more you listen and learn, then the more your language grows to accommodate its new needs.

But always write what you want to read.

Never write what you wouldn't want to read if you hadn't written it.

•

EXTINCT LANGUAGES, A Sampler.

| | |
|---|---|
| Egyptian Hieroglyphics | Hurrian |
| Meroitic Script | Urartaean |
| Persian Cuneiform | Ugaritic |
| Sumerian | Lycian |
| Non-Elamite | Side |
| Babylonian | Numidian |
| Hittite | Etruscan |
| Cognate | Phrygian |
| Sinaitic Script | Cretan-Minoan Script |
| Carian | Indus Valley Script |

—Gleaned from *Extinct Languages*
by Johannes Friedrich. Philosophical
Library, New York, 1957

•

# PART FOUR

PARTS, OF

*Parts, 1*

How many words does a poem have to have to be a poem?
Whatever it takes.
You may quote me.
Whatever it takes to make the poem the poem you want
it to be. That's how many words.

•

*Parts, 2 [with a problem]*

Words are made up of sounds assembled in clusters like music. A word can have one or more tones to it.

When you say "alto saxophone" or "ukulele" you are producing a kind of song.

Lullabies use words that soothe.

TV commercials are composed of special word-tones that induce you to leap out of bed or off the floor or out of the vinyl easy-chair and run down the block to the shopping center to buy a box of mini-pad Kotex for a wife you plan to have someday.

Jazz singers sometimes take the words out of a song and substitute sounds which make the song sound more like a jazz solo on a trumpet than the telling of a lyric.

And there are more uses of sound-tones that you can think of. And you should. It's interesting to sit in your backyard and try and locate in your vast memory the uses of sound-tones in language. Or, better yet, just sit in your backyard and relax.

But, the problem I'm interested in having you solve is this:

Show me a poem with silence in it. Describe silence.

•

## Additional Problems

### 1.

Write a love poem that doesn't mention the word "love" or any of its synonyms.

Make love an actual presence in the poem, a fact.

### 2.

Write a hate poem, a diatribe, that doesn't mention the word "hate" or any of its synonyms and, if possible, a poem that doesn't mention contemporary or historical world leaders and/or politicians.

### 3.

Write a mystical visionary poem without mentioning the word "God" or "Buddha" or "Wotan" etc., without mentioning the invisible, the ineffable, the beyond, the within, without mentioning angels or devils, wheels, hexes, *vévés,* holy holy.

Write a mystical visionary poem without using any of the language usually associated with so-called devotional poetry.

Make a mystical visionary poem emerge from the clearly stated facts of your own reality.

Invent new symbols, new words, to express and define your mystical and visionary values; write rituals out of materials gathered from the spot you stand on. Write on the spot. The right rite.

### 4.

Describe pain without showing it, without describing the wound.

5.

Write a two-line poem that states accurately everything you know in the time it takes to write a two-line poem.

•

Other problems will follow.

•

Accept, expect, your limits. Explore them.

The poem is a record of that process.

No matter how small, as a haiku or couplet or aphorism, no matter how large, as an epic or serial poem, a limit is agreed upon and the poem and poet work within these limits.

Even the page we work on is an agreement of limit.

The poem remains limitless.

·

Punctuation.
A way of notation, cantillation.
You may or may not use
commas,
or semi-colons;
or colons:
or dots . . .
or dashes—
(or brackets)
or "explanation marks"
or asterisks * * *
or ? question marks ?
or slashes / /
or you may or may not use any punctuation at all.
You learn as you read and as you write about which devices most suit your poem's purpose.

•

*Parts, 4*

> *Me no know,*
> *Me no care,*
> *Push a button,*
> *And go somewhere.*
>
> (Children's street song, U.S.)

•

*No mo textbooks*
*No mo how-to*
*If you don't want to,*
*Have to,*
*You'll never*
*Ever.*

(Graffiti)

•

*Suicide*

A b c d e f
g h i j k l
m n o p q r
s t u v w
x y z

—Louis Aragon (c. 1922)

The length of each line in a poem helps to create what is called "measure." The poem's measure, its beat, is the poem's pivot. It gives the words a momentum.

Meter, measure. The poem's time signature, the poet's signature, his imprint.

Every poet struggles to one degree or another with rhythm. It's a paradoxically balanced effort. You learn how to allow the poem its rhythm while, at the same time, you impose your own particular sense of rhythm onto it.

Jazz musicians know that you cannot begin to improvise effectively until you've mastered rhythms. The poet also learns to work within and around the rhythms in his poem and to give proportion to the tonal potential of his vocabulary.

Words like notes have a tonal weight. (But that deserves a section to itself.)

Punctuation, word-tone, line length, all aid in maintaining the poem's rhythm power.

•

*Parts, 6*

A stanza is like a paragraph is in prose.
It's a row of words that stops
When a thought is stopped
In order to give you space to
Think about it.

Or a stanza can be
more of a

way to
get you to

a sense of
the poem's voice,

its rhythm
or speech.
In space

or across the
blank face

I type black
insults against.

•

A stanza can be one or two or three or four or fifty or one hundred lines long.

A stanza can be a word.

Any poem is like a painting. It's built up out of parts. Strokes, layers, surfaces, textures, forms that interrelate and balance and together create a whole entity.

•

Voice. One always hears: "He hasn't found his voice yet." "You've got to find your own voice."

Voice is essence, a fact distinguishing one poet's work from another. A quality which makes work immediately recognized.

It will always be a mystery and a frustration to those of us unable to accomplish from our own resources that which seems so effortless in others.

Voice. It is what it is. Unmistakable. A rarity. Nobody can possess it, no matter how they try.

•

Never feel dishonest or dishonorable for trying on the master's robes. It is an essential ritual. But remember not to wear them too long and begin to think they're yours. They will swallow you up. And that will be that.

•

# PART FIVE

*We must remember, however, that art is of value only to the extent that it speaks to us. It might be a universal language if we ourselves were universal in our sympathies.*

—Kakuzo Okakura

I asked Jenny how she knew what she saw in the mirror was really what she looked like.

An answer began to part her lips, but in mid-breath she stopped and shook her head.

—What do you mean? she asked.

We laughed about it.

·

It's no different with your poem on the page. How do you know what you wanted to say is what you've written?

·

The art of art, the glory of expression and the sunshine of the light of letters is simplicity. Nothing is better than simplicity . . . nothing can make up for excess or the lack of definiteness. To carry on the heave of impulse and pierce intellectual depths and give all subjects their articulations are powers neither common nor very uncommon. But to speak in literature with the perfect rectitude and insouciance of the movements of animals and the unimpeachableness of the sentiment of trees in the woods and the grass by the roadside is the flawless triumph of art. If you have looked on him who has achieved it you have looked on one of the masters of the artists of all nations and times. You shall not contemplate the flight of the graygull over the bay or the mettlesome action of the blood horse or the tall leaning of sunflowers on their stalk or the appearance of the sun journeying through heaven or the appearance of the moon afterward with any more satisfaction than you shall contemplate him. The greatest poet has less a marked style and is more the channel of thoughts and things without increase or diminution, and is the free channel of himself. He swears to his art, I will not be meddlesome, I will not have in my writing any elegance or effect or originality to hang in the way between me and the rest like curtains. I will have nothing hang in the way, not the richest curtains. What I tell I tell for precisely what it is. Let who may exalt or startle or fascinate or soothe, I will have purposes as health or heat or snow has and be regardless of observation. What I experience or portray shall go from my composition without a shred of my composition. You shall stand by my side and look in the mirror with me.

—Walt Whitman

•

A poem is a two-way mirror.

•

"Moving or allowing movement in either direction."

•

A poem is how the poet looks out at you. His words make you look back upon the page to see yourself revealed.

A recognition.

•

The poem is a two-way mirror concealing a page.

•

A poet sees what you see but brings back the image in words that makes the seeing more memorable and always within reach.

The emotions a poem restores reflect back to you.

A recognition you can use to reach back into the meaning of a moment that had passed.

A poem is a two-way mirror.

You must look into it in order to see, to recognize your own face.

No one ever knows in a one-way mirror what they really look like.

•

A poem is a two-way mirror means more than a one-way mirror—even though both mean possibilities of seeing.

In a one-way mirror the image is stopped. In a two-way mirror the image "moves, allows movement in either direction."

In a one-way mirror the glass aspects only a portion of what we look into to see. Glass is a reflecting surface. (Glass is a poem.)

As you notice, I prefer poems that are two-way mirrors.

•

"Beauty is only skin deep."

•

A poem is a two-way mirror also means this:

You are recalled to profound feelings brought back by a poem.

A poem allows you sight of what is on the surface as well as what is beneath the surface or behind it or beyond it. Like a two-way mirror.

A poem restores your world to a level of revelation.

If not that, a poem can at least open you up to the possibility of using the page as a mirror.

"Revelation" means something seen completely.

"I *see* the Light!"

Revelation can be as big or as small as your capacity to contain it.

That's why there is such a range of poetry available to any person seeking it.

•

A poem is a two-way mirror—*mirror, mirror, on the wall* —as in the fantasy, turns into a well, the well a road through time the imagination speeds across. Fast glance at gone familiar faces, sounds of conversation fragments, old songs, jingles, people who do not recognize you, turning away, movie world, television world, faces reassemble into dots holding together newspaper photographs—a catalog of seen and unseen joys and sorrows in the moment of your gazing—existing in the self museum, invoked by a poem whose page is a mirror.

•

It is likewise probable that the pre-ecstatic euphoria constituted one of the universal sources of lyric poetry. In preparing his trance, the shaman drums, summons his spirit helpers, speaks a "secret" language or the "animal language," imitating the cries of beasts and especially the songs of birds. He ends by obtaining a "second state" that provides the impetus for linguistic creation and the rhythms of lyric poetry. Poetic creation still remains an act of perfect spiritual freedom. Poetry remakes and prolongs language; every poetic language begins by being a secret language, that is, the creation of a personal universe, of a completely closed world. The purest poetic act seems to re-create language from an inner experience that, like ecstasy or the religious inspiration or "primitives," reveals the essence of things. It is from such linguistic creations, made possible by pre-ecstatic "inspiration," that the "secret languages" of the mystics and the traditional allegorical languages later crystalize.

—Mircea Eliade

•

The ancient Poets animated all sensible objects with Gods or Geniuses, calling them by the names and adorning them with the properties of woods, rivers, mountains, lakes, cities, nations, and whatever their enlarged and numerous senses could perceive.

And particularly they studied the genius of each city and country, placing it under its mental deity.

Till a system was formed, which some took advantage of and enslav'd the vulgar by attempting to realize the abstract the mental deities from their objects; thus began Priesthood.

Choosing forms of worship from poetic tales.

And at length they pronounced that the Gods had ordered such things.

Thus men forgot that All deities reside in the human breast.

—William Blake

•

Poetry does not yet exist. Words are brought out one by one, placed on a page. Then they are read (silently) (into the silence), tested and outlined against the object and creatures present. Those that cannot be substituted for states or actions of living or inanimate things are considered subversive to clarity of thought. So far the most advanced form of prosody is considered to be the list.

—Clark Coolidge

•

**THIS IS ROY G. BIV**
Can you remember his name? If you can, you will be able to remember the colors that make up sunlight—

      Red
      Orange
      Yellow

      Green

      Blue
      Indigo
      Violet

## One

Poetry of faith. The inside turned outside. Numinous moments re-translated into words.

Tombstones studded with angels.

Singing telegrams from God.

## Two

Poetry of landscape. The outside turned inside turned outside again.

They are like paintings. Either vertical like Chinese or Japanese scrolls or horizontal on the canvas page like Cézanne.

Painting with words, describing what's seen. Trying to make the reader see beyond what is seen. Like Eastern or Western masters, a poet tries to place himself in proper perspective on the page.

## Three

Inscape poetry. The inside turned inside-out like the lining of a coat. Or a Moebius strip.

Abstract, meditational.

No image, no face. Mostly concepts, thoughts.

Word quilt. Symbols wearing cement shoes, slinking and clunking about, debating on the meaning of meaning. Dictionary spaghetti.

## Four

Words as words. Alone. Themselves. Disconnected.

Page a space where words are placed at random and the reader has to deal with each word on its own terms.

As in concrete poems or sound poems. Minimal. Non-linear. Beads. Sparks.

Either the acme of refinement or the white flag.

## Five

Pick-up-sticks. In this case, words.

Mallarmé announced it: *Un coup de dés jamais n'abolira le hasard.* A throw of the dice will never abolish chance.

Automatic writing, which has nothing at all to do with machinery or pistols.

It is a way of writing without thinking about what you are writing.

It means not exerting conscious control over what comes forth and letting what the page holds stand for the work which wanted to be there.

It is being a vessel or conduit for the poem.

Some say it is a way to turn your head into a Niagara of language you spill all over rising piles of pages.

•

In the 1950s Jack Kerouac called it Spontaneous Bop Prosody. During the 1920s when James Joyce was working the hardest it was called Stream of Consciousness.

Recently Allen Ginsberg paraphrased Buddha and told a group of poets that "first thought is best thought."

Jack Spicer taught us that the poet is a receiver like a

radio that poems come through and the poet transfers the message to paper.

Then some say that nothing is automatic, spontaneous. No matter how fast the speed of light, a poet will always be a micro-second ahead of it, sorting and editing, juggling and weighing, arranging the waterfall into a beautiful and constant shape.

•

# Six

So far, the revolutionary poem by definition and usage cannot be a literary event. Propaganda rarely strives to be art. The revolutionary poem uses the page as an expedient. It would rather be in the air like a song that everyone can sing loudly as a source of strength and solidarity. It's meant as an inspired order to action. It serves a moment in history and becomes a part of the past. Or it becomes a national anthem. But then even its power remains in the past and to those who live in the past.

There is rarely an individual stamp to a revolutionary poem; there are no soloists, no virtuosi, because it is a poem trying to reach a large body of people in a direct manner. It strives to sing in the voice of the people it is addressed to. There is no romance or beauty about poverty, racism, or nationalism.

A revolutionary poem should be as blunt and unavoidable as the revolution it asks for. There should be no way around its message. It must be written in a voice that won't shut off, even after you've closed the book.

•

## Seven

The casual poem.

They seem easy to write becasue they're so easy to read. But don't be deceived.

The best of them are examples of how a poet learns to say enough.

They can be about anything. Everything has value if the poet wishes to give it value. Clipping your toenails can be a poem. Making a pot of coffee. Every inch we live in can be a poem.

The casual poem is usually extremely short. Sometimes two lines, maybe even one.

As a form it is not new at all. Perhaps it started in ancient Greece or in China. The *Greek Anthology* or Sapphic fragments or *Carmina Archilochi*; or Egyptian fragments or Chinese epigrams. Statements of a momentary fact. After all, a poem doesn't have to fill a volume or even a page. It can, according to you, be a big deal or not so big a deal.

Casual poems often have no notion of immortality. Very modest. Often funny and usually *au courant.* Metaphysical graffiti. Kilroy was here. Etc.

Breezy snapshots from the city or the country—wherever the poet hangs his eyes.

Poetry is a part of a person's life and cannot be withdrawn from it, isolated so that it becomes something more than the person, something bigger than the person, like religion or a mystery.

But, then again.

•

# PART SIX

## *FROM THE WORD-BOOK*

The word. You say it slow enough and two birds' wings flutter out of your mouth.

The word. I've said it loud enough to make you cry.

The word. She never said it, not even on her deathbed.

The word. He looked for it through every library in the world.

•

We are talking, but not together.

To speak together would mean the same voice, the same words, while we both move our mouths together against the air of a room.

We are talking about God.

You say it is an energy, it is manifest in light.

When I think of energy, I think of Niagara Falls whose energy is manifest in electricity which lights the lights above our heads.

You say God is a word we clothe the invisible with. We dress what we cannot see in words.

Does the invisible speak to you?

No. You say it speaks through you.

Now I know the secret of words.

•

There's this scientist.

He lives in a University and has a laboratory and spends most of his time being paid to look for the roots of words.

They keep drilling deeper into the earth to get to the end and beginning of things.

At this moment, his laboratory takes a week to reach the last floor.

There is one machine he is very proud of. It's an egg-shaped crystal a word gave birth to in another machine they do not show civilians.

The egg-shaped crystal has a light in its center. This light, says the scientist, is the secret of all words.

Now I know the secret exists.

It's comforting that there are so many people working on its decipherment.

•

Dear Jim,

Want me to tell you what the mystery of poetry is?

Can't do it. I mean, it can't be done.

One, it's no mystery. Two, a lie.

Three, there is no theory. Four, I lie.

Five, I invent everything that does and doesn't exist.

Six, no lie.

Seven and/or eleven. We know those numbers well. But I'm still broke.

Eight, the secret of poetry is never told.

Nine, I lie.

Ten, wanna read my newest poem?

Open the door and shut your eyes.

•

I've always said that Gertrude Stein and Wittgenstein were chips off the old block.

The old block is cement and I lived on it in Brooklyn. There I was taught all I know about language. It's heavy to carry a house on your back. Especially if it's an apartment.

Gertrude Stein and Wittgenstein supplied each other with esoteric information that is completely indispensible.

All of their books tell you that poetry is no mystery.

All of their books affirm the mystery.

Nobody lies.

Then again, nobody tells the truth.

Tell the truth to pick up a pint of half-&-half for me, since he's going to the store.

•

A word I like is "ontological." Almost as much as "phenomenological."

But I don't like the word "logical" which ends both of the above-mentioned words.

"Logical" is a shut door. When I'm hitting below the belt in an argument with my wife, I accuse her of being logical. It's a condemnation, a damnation.

Wipe that logical smirk off your smarmy mug.

I also like the word "smarmy."

"Mug" is an affectation, a longing for the past. It's a word that's a French translation into English into French of an American word popular in the 1920s. Both W.R. Burnett and Blaise Cendrars are also fond of the word.

Spelled backwards it is gum. That's what mugs are always chewing in their big traps.

•

How I analyze the Ideogram.
"Career."
Ka-Rear.
Ka, the shadow; rear, the end.
So, career is the shadow of your end.
Next.

•

For that matter I also like the name of the English poet William Wordsworth.

What an absolutely correct poet's name. Wordsworth.

So evocative of what it is, in the beginning or end, all about.

•

I spend half of my life with just a few words. A few words. How many others do you know who spend half their life with just a few words?

These words keep coming back, just as I seem to keep coming back to them.

We meet in the middle of the street and embrace each other like old friends. There is still so much left to say.

•

Michael Wiater brings these words into our house: Minimal Art and Conceptual Art.

But when they're said and done, what we really talk most interestedly on is the *brujo*'s art.

The conversation returns again and again to Don Juan, to Castañeda, to how every one of us is forced to speak for or against the words on a page in a book.

•

If the word fits. A million parables about it.

How a seeker sought the truth. How he went into the cave of inward seasons. How he returned after years of contemplation, his beard white.

Now I know it. Now I know that it is beyond words, said the seeker becoming the teacher.

Tell us more, they asked.

He did.

He hasn't stopped.

He's still at it.

His 22nd book in 10 years has been announced for spring publication. It's called *The Unspeakable*, a sequel to his last book, *Beyond Words*.

•

Words get in the way of what is.

For instance, the bamboo in the backyard. Just seeing it refreshes my senses. Describing it is another matter. I've worked days on a poem that attempts to catch the aura of its green grace. But the words get in the way.

In the way of what?

In the way of what is, in the way of what isn't. Either way they get in the way.

Yet they are the only way out, the only way in.

·

There is always the delusion or illusion about how to read. It has to do with whether or not you read the white or the black. Whether the black was really there all the time, built into each piece of white paper.

•

After I read my poems the questions begin.

Many want to know what happens when I write a poem. They want a secret that nobody listens to.

How do you write a poem, what happens?

Once I pulled the zipper down from the neck to the genitals and reached in and pulled out a wall-map which I hung over the blackboard.

With a pointer I touched many zones and spheres which somehow or other interconnect, from moment to moment, to fuel the event which is the writing of a poem.

I didn't have much time to explain because many in the crowd began to scream and point wildly at the waterfall of blood pouring out of my wide-open body.

•

So, what is it you want from the master?
Someone to take charge of your life?
Someone to guide you through all chaos?
Someone to restore your pride yet sustain your habits?

These are some of the questions I scribble down in my homework book.

Don't ask me any questions.
I'm not the master.

•

## The Night School

This is a night school.

Men and women go to this school. They have friends here. The men and women in this school see their friends here.

The teacher took some good books from the school library and gave them to the men and women. The teacher keeps these books and some paper in a small room in the school.

---

NEW WORDS: night picture teacher

---

# PART SEVEN

*PARDES*

## THE BARDS' ENIGMA

*There is nothing truly hidden but what is not conceivable;*
*There is nothing conceivable but what is immeasurable;*
*There is nothing immeasureable but God;*
*There is no God but that which is not conceivable;*
*There is nothing not conceivable but that which is truly*
     *hidden;*
*There is nothing truly hidden but God.*

—From *Barddas*

•

*Pardes is the symbolic and mystical garden in Kabbalah, containing the supreme knowledge of the Creator and creation. It requires great courage to enter the Garden. . . .*

*The legend tells us of the four* Tanaim[1] *who entered the Garden: Rabbi Ben Azai, Ben Zoma, Elisha ben Avuah and Rabbi Akiba.*

*Ben Azai gazed at the Garden and died.*

*Ben Zoma looked upon it and lost his senses.*

*Elisha ben Avuah began to cut the trees down and became a heretic.*

*Only Rabbi Akiba entered the Garden in peace and left the Garden in peace.*

From the Talmud

•

*Four persons entered the* Pardes [*orchard*] [*the study of theosophic speculation of the Gnostic, concerning the nature of the Godhead, the process of Creation, and the Mystery of Evil*]. *These were: Ben Azzai, Ben Zoma,* Aher[2] [*the surname given to Elisha ben Abuyah*], *and Rabbi Akiba. Ben Zoma cast a look and died at an early age; Ben Azzai cast a look and became demented; Elisha ben Abuyah cut down the plants of the Torah* [*became*

---

1. *Tanaim*, an Aramaic word meaning "one who studies and teaches"—especially the oral law. The period of the *tanaim* began after Hillel and Shammai and ended with the generation after Rabbi Judah ha-Nasi in the 2nd Century C.E.; thus the last generations of the *tanaim* lived after the destruction of the Second Temple.

2. *Aher*—"that other one." Despite his great learning, he became estranged from Judaism. Rabbi Meir, who had been his disciple, remained loyal to him throughout life. When the question at the academy was asked, why he continued to seek learning from the mouth of *Aher*, the reply was: "Rabbi Meir found a pomegranate—he ate the inner part, but cast away its shell" (Hagigah, 15b).

*estranged from Judaism], and Rabbi Akiba alone emerged in peace. The Mishnah [Sotah, 9] states: "With the passing of Ben Zoma, there were no more expounders [of the Torah]."*

•

*Pardes* or *PaRDeS* is a word and an anagram describing a method of reading texts. It is also a method of inquiry. The four stages of the anagram were specifically used as an approach to the full dimension of Judaism's primary sacred text, the Torah. Yet the anagram's progressions can also be very well used in reading or writing poetry. Or, for that matter, in any text demanding complete attention.

The word *pardes* is transliterated from the Hebrew and directly means "garden" or "orchard" or "Paradise." It is a word which also has bearing to the Greek *paradeisos*.

The anagram of the word is created through a method of condensation called *notarikon*, where the letters of a word are taken to be the initials of yet another word, or as an abbreviation of a phrase, stanza or passage from the Torah or any number of Jewish holy books.

The anagram presents a process of increasing recognition in four grades or planes or perception.

*Pa* = *P'shat*, the simple and literal meaning: what is is what is.

*R* = *Remez*, the deductive meaning, what is intimated: what is is not necessarily what it seems to be.

*De* = *Deresh*, the inductive meaning with an emphasis on homiletic interpretation.

*S* = *Sod*, "secret," the esoteric reading.

•

Each letter-word exists on its own level. The process is like the poem and is one step at a time.

There are no limits as to how long we must dwell in any of the planes. Expanded knowledge leads us to the next step.

Some say that the process of PaRDeS is circular and that it invariably returns to the beginning—which is the simple, the literal.

•

*Jack and Jill went up the hill*
*To fetch a pail of water.*
*Jack fell down and broke his crown*
*And Jill came tumbling after.*

*P'shat:*—It is what it says it is. No more, no less. A simple rhyme with the sequential clarity of a newspaper story.

*Remez:*—Geography is absent. What hill, where?

Why did they go up the hill in the first place? Was there actually a well there, or was the pail of water sitting there waiting to be fetched? Was it a magic place or one of evil and entrapment? How did the pail of water get there?

What season was it? Was it winter, which would have made the hill treacherous with frozen grass?

Was it day or night? What time was it?

Were Jack and Jill brother and sister or husband and wife or were they components of one person?

Is Jill the feminine element released after the "crown" is broken? (The Crown being *Kether*, which is directly aligned with *Tiphereth* [Beauty], *Yesod* [Foundation], *Malkuth* [Kingdom].) In the Tree of Life structure their numerical values are 1, 6, 9, and 10, which, added together, yield the number 26, whose parts add to 8, which is the numerical value of the Hebrew letter *Cheth*, which signifies an enclosure or fence, which returns us to the "crown." Also, the number 8 can be divided into two 4's, which could indicate two Tetragrammatons, which could indicate the God (life-creation energy) within each person and could, therefore, be symbolic of Jack and Jill as two individuals as well as part of the Almighty One.

*Deresh*:—The method which indicates that everything isn't what it looks like or seems to be and reinforces that conclusion with an example culled from an old book:

<br>

Wherein,
a young man and his new and foolish bride are given a most spectacular wedding and receive opulent and bountiful presents from relatives, friends, neighbors and well-wishers. But the new bride isn't happy with her gifts. She feels that there should be more. Ever since she was born, she has always wanted more and more. This strange craving is the result of a curse delivered to the new bride's mother when she was pregnant. It was manufactured and uttered by a man with strange green eyes, yellow teeth and a disarming stump where his left leg should be.

"More, more," she whines to her husband. "There must be more."

Her new husband despairs and reluctantly tells her of Gorman The Dark, his unspoken of and unspoken to (extremely unpopular) Great Uncle.

"If we go to him," shudders the husband, "he will make us wealthy beyond measure."

"Let's go now," snaps the greedy new wife.

"But, darling, sweetheart, tender toes, Great Uncle Gorman The Dark will make us pay dearly for everything. You must understand how vicious and hateful and . . ."

"I'll hear no more. We must leave immediately."

"But what about our honeymoon?" the new groom groans.

"It will just have to wait until after we return from Great Uncle Gorman The Dark's."

Off they go.

Up and down high and low roads. In and out of lit and un-lit tunnels. Through woods, out of woods. Along floors of narrow canyons, silhouettes of grim birds flying above them. Into dank forests smelling of poisoned mushrooms. Out of dank forests into sudden corroding tropic sunlight. Across lakes where sharp-toothed sucking underwater menaces cling to their ankles and knees and the young man almost loses his big toe to an insidious crab shaped like a crusty andiron. Out of lakes onto shores of burning sand which harden into glass splinters. Across rocky paths where gruesome trees grow gnarled and bent. Macabre. Frozen branches cut and gash and whip across the seekers' tender cheeks.

On and on and on.

And at each more forbidding place, the young man implores his new wife to return.

His new wife shakes her head and bellows loud and clear, "We've come this far, we're not going back. What kind of a clod and nitwit have I married? Onward to Great Uncle Gorman The Dark's palaces of gold and silver and jewels and riches beyond belief!"

(You're welcome to improvise additional unpleasant details of their trip. In the old book there are endless pages depicting hideous nasty demeaning events befalling the young couple. No matter what, the greedy bride will not be daunted. She keeps reminding her haggard and utterly pale husband, "You lump of crud, you promised me everything!

You said there was nothing you wouldn't give me: the sun, the moon, the stars! Feh! I want Jewels and gold and silver and stuff and more stuff! Be true to your word you crumbling crock of snot!" . . . There are at least four or five long detailed chapters of the same before they finally arrive at the grotesquely shaped mouth of a cave. This is the entrance to Gorman's underground estate. The couple immediately enters the misshapen mouth of the cave.)

It takes them four days and four nights to reach bottom where they're sullenly greeted by blind smelly hulks who are Gorman The Dark's servants. Bumping about a lot, they manage to guide the couple into the innermost lair to meet, at last, Great Uncle Gorman The Dark.

Uncle Gorman The Dark spends the next two and a half chapters thoroughly and ultimately denouncing the young groom for being birthed into a family of cosmic deadbeats. "Scurrilous wretched stick-in-the-muds! Heads-in-the-sand! Noses-in-the-air! Incompetents! Droolers! Low-life low-brow loathsome family! *Argh, argh, argh!* How did *I* ever manage to be born into such a pudding of good-for-nothings? Such a rancid vulgar stew of losers and bamboozlers!"

Gorman curses them all. The living, the dead, the yet-to-be-born.

It goes on for a week while the young couple stand in respectful silence.

The cave reeks of rottenness. Mulched bowels. Decomposed oceans. A nauseating fire sparkles, crackles, belches, burbles, pops off unsavory chunks of indescribable substances against the murky cave walls. The muck is stenched with smudge and grey-green smog. All of it tinted in B-movie puce.

Ever since he was thrown out of the family, Gorman The Dark has thought of nothing else but avenging and revenging his name. Before making his enormous fortune, he spent years pleasing his loathsome heartless soul by cursing pregnant women, cursing their unborn children into living insidious memory of Gorman The Dark's revenge. No need to continue. The book provides us with two endings, neither really satisfying:

1) Great Uncle Gorman The Dark intuitively senses the results of one of his curses in the shape of the new bride and is satisfied. In fact, he is so satisfied that this odious female has wed into his cursed scurvy family that he becomes approximately sentimental. Irony, it turns out, brings the fires to his heart. He orders a troupe of hulks and heaps to wheel out a wagon filled with gold and silver and jewels. The wagon lights up the funky murk with a neon dazzle. Facets flash and splash lights all over the cave's walls. (Which actually makes the place look even more ghastly and gut-knotting.)

"Here," grumbles Uncle Gorman The Dark, "take this wagon away and return in haste to your muzzy home."

"Is that all?" screeches the new bride. "Why isn't there more?"

"What do you mean?" barks Gorman The Dark.

"Is that all of your jewels and gold and silver? Dammit, man, is this *really* all your *stuff*!!?"

Great Uncle Gorman The Dark smiles mysteriously, which is a very uncomfortable thing to see.

"It's more than enough," he answers, folding his hairy arms across his hairy chest and steadying the twitching stump of his left leg.

"What are you talking about? Nothing is ever enough!" demands the young greedy bride, the tendons on her neck bulging against her skin.

"Every step you take away from this place will cause all the gold and silver and jewels to multiply. . . ."

The new bride squeals in gleeful greed, her eyes become bright as newly minted gold coins.

"But," warns Gorman, "you'll not be able to remove any of the gold or silver or jewels until you return to your home . . . or else it will all disappear and you will be struck dead on the spot!"

"Ohhhh," groans the bridegroom, knowing his time and strength are gone.

The author(s) of the text insist upon adding a moral to the story's first ending: "Never make promises you can't keep."

2) Gorman The Dark sees much that is pleasantly familiar in the greedy young bride and reasons that it would be best (and just) to claim her as his ally.

The bridegroom puts up little argument. He coyly reminds his mercenary bride that he did, indeed, promise her everything, and "everything" turns out to be Great Uncle Gorman The Dark.

She doesn't say goodbye nor does she embrace her new seedy besmirched mate, instead she gallops off to the myriad treasure rooms vaulted in Gorman's lair. Before committing herself to anything, she wants to take complete inventory of all the goods and treasures stored in Gorman The Dark's world.

•

—That's it?

—That's it.

—But what about the last step, the fourth plane?

—Ah, yes. *Sod:*—mystery, esoteric significance. One aspect I can reveal about the *PaRDeS* process revealed in these pages: the first few pages of the text I have just written were first written in a dream. As I was writing what I thought to be a new work, a sudden flashback opened its book to remind me that I'd already written these same words in a dream several weeks earlier.

·

PART EIGHT

*SUB-MINIMAL MAXIMS*

*—I have a lady
in the balcony, Doctor…*

No subject is more or less "poetic." Despite the clanking echoes of what many of us have learned, poetry can be about anything and still be poetry. You don't have to write love poems. You don't have to write poems about how vast the sea and sky are. Poems don't have to rise off the page like ornate Victorian Zeppelins fired with romance and rhetoric. You write about whatever you think or feel deserves or wants a poem.

•

All loved ones are extremely pleased to know that their lovers pay attention to them as individuals and as real persons. Who started the rumor that love poems have to be vague?

•

Make every inch of your beloved into a poem. Watch out for words that embalm. Love is always now. Mourning is later.

•

Stravinsky said this about technique:

"The whole man. We learn how to use it but we can not acquire it in the first place; or, perhaps, I should say we were born with the ability to acquire it. At present it has come to mean the opposite of 'heart,' though, of course, 'heart' is technique too. . . . 'Thought' is not one thing and then 'technique' another, namely, the ability to transfer, 'express,' or develop thoughts. We cannot say 'the technique of Bach' (I never say it), yet in every sense he had more of it than anyone; our extraneous meaning becomes ridiculous when we try to imagine the separation of Bach's musical substance and the making of it. Technique is not a teachable science, neither is it learning, nor scholarship, nor even the knowledge of how to do something. It is creation, and, being creation, it is new every time."

•

Poems start inside and work their way out. Or they are outside and work their way in.

However it happens, you have to be ready for it.

A poem can be an angel singing with your mouth, or it can be a banana slug on the rose bush and you don't know whether to kill it or not. Sometimes the banana slug on the rose bush will sing to you the song of an angel. But that's another matter. We are talking about where poems come from.

Outside and they work their way in; inside and they work their way out.

It's also possible that a poem comes from both places at the same time and collide head-on. You have to be ready to reassemble the parts.

•

Everyone wants to know where poems come from and I can't really tell them.

In the moment of creating, there's nothing there except the potential of your intelligence, feelings and imagination. Writing is the process of using yourself to the fullest capacity.

Poems come from everywhere.

•

7.   This is a station.
8.   The man in the station gives a ticket to that man.
9.   The ticket is in his hand.
10.  The man in the station gives a ticket to that woman.
11.  The ticket is in her hand.

REVIEW WORDS: hand gives to

Try everything.

Use the poem in all of the ways you can invent to use it.

Sing in all the voices you have. Rhyme or not. It's always up to you.

Try all the forms that interest you. Learn what works.

Try none of the forms and, instead, shape a form most usable for your own sense of song.

Remember: the forms were there for specific use in specific times when poetry had a special value each age must declare anew.

Try* everything at least once. Like hats, see what fits you best.

•

---

* Additional meanings of "try." *Trying*, or to *try*, refers to a process of purifying, or refinement. When they melt down whale blubber for oil, that's called "trying-out." Also: to "try out" means to audition for a part. Try the poems. Try-out your poems. Try-out for the poem. Try-umph. *Selah.*

This making of a poem is a mystery, a paradox, a matter of sitting down and doing it, paying attention, being present, learning all over again what you know.

The illumination arrived at is always something we already knew deep down in one of the amazing chambers of our ordinary selves. But why we are poets in continual journey back and forth from known to known is because we demand the process of going to the source, returning to it, being able to recognize its face and form again and again. Some of us can spend a lifetime with one truth trying to tell it right. Cocteau said you had to be tenacious to be a poet. Stubborn, tough, often literal, dogged to the point of exasperation. The paper turns away from our bleak stare. Wives and children vanish from our zombie stalking through the house in search of the exact replica of truth the page conceals from us. Lovers cannot see or hear us, we have transformed ourselves beyond love's immediate realms. Pursuing some fine point, perhaps a comma or, more likely, the specific word which will balance one entire three-line poem.

•

Art clarifies, it doesn't simplify.

Even the most primitive song-maker gave birth to song out of complex maneuvers.

You've got to train for poetry just like all the other arts, just like anything, even sleep. It's as simple as that. You have to be in shape. Alert, responsive. Come out fighting.

The more you know, the easier it is to cut through the grease.

The less you know, the fatter your head gets.

Doors close, windowshades drawn. Dark times.

•

I have been talking about two essential and primary poetries: the inward and the outward.

Visible poems, outward poems, move across the page like light on water.

Invisible poems, inward poems, ignite internal lights, illuminate and expand the self-territory.

Both forms of poem function as agents of change within a reader.

One poem attempts to order what is. The other attempts to give order to the invisible, to give it shape and actuality.

One is on the line.

The other is between the lines.

•

Many are led to mystery; others to reality.

The poem has the possibility of showing how each can become the other.

The "mystery" is what goes on while you are creating.

It seems to be above the parts you are moving on the page. The parts that you move are also moving you. During those instants of sorting words, images, emotions, the mystery remains like a dome above you.

The mystery is the context we work inside of. We are surrounded by the circle of our vision.

•

From a papyrus fragment:
    *Grounding*
    *Or*
    *Grinding*
    *As it is with lenses.*

---

COMMENTARY: Another way of seeing through or to or at the poem as well as the process of writing the poem.

"Grounding" indicates placement, level, center, presence.

"Grinding" indicates process, bearing down, carving away, working into, working with, extracting, condensing.

"Lenses" are what poems are. We wear them for our eyes, we look through them.

•

My poems are often abbreviations. I try to boil away the fat.

My best poems are usually hungry and graceful and alert. They dance on the edges of invisibility; they are inevitable.

My bad poems are fat, loud and sloppy. They stumble around like drunk cossacks trying to dance in the freeway during rush-hour.

•

There's a useful analogy between "hungry" and "full" in the making and considering of a poem.

When you're hungry your senses seem to operate more completely. They become roots growing closer to each moment.

But when you've stuffed your gut, your senses shut off. You become a stomach and that's all. You turn on the TV and hope it will put you to sleep.

It's wise therefore to always be a little hungry.

"Fathead" is a very apt word.

•

### Second Lesson

1. This is a man.

2. This is a bag.

3. That is his bag.

4. That bag is his bag.

---

NEW WORDS: his her bag

---

When I first came to Los Angeles I worked for an old Jewish woman who owned an open-air newsstand at the corner of Hollywood Boulevard and Western Avenue.

It was an ideal job for a culture-shocked 16-year-old kid from Brooklyn. All the magazines, pocketbooks, comicbooks, girlie-books, newspapers, pulp, trash and kitsch I could read. I also had free rein over candybars, chewing gum and cigarettes. It was no wonder I stayed on the job for over a year instead of going back to high school.

Like a bookstore, a magazine stand attracts a special type of person, people who enjoy the company of typography, who are comforted by print. Some of my regular and best customers were pimps, homosexuals, undercover cops, opera singers (and the parents of opera singers), dope pushers, gamblers, tapdancers, extras, yogis, prophets, mystics, psychics, magicians, gangsters, iconoclasts, anarchists, and so on. But no more lists.

One man used to come every day for the scratch-sheets. He was small, tanned to a crisp, with thinning hair, thick glasses, and there was always a cigarette either hanging off his lower lip or squeezed between his thumb and forefinger, held out like a movie version of a Russian count. (George Sanders or Paul Lukas held cigarettes that way in certain key movies.)

He talked to me about the book he was writing. It was going to be the ultimate work on the art and science of handicapping horse races. Not just a run-of-the-mill, hit-or-miss effort, but *the* masterwork to transcend and discourage all future attempts.

—How's it done ? I asked.

—By numbers and stars, he answered. —By the theory of correspondences and how things relate to each other: star to star, planet to planet, star to horse. Horses, yknow, are very lunar. I take everything into account.

All of which sounded fine to me. I told him that I thought he must have spent a great deal of time studying the stars, the horses, the moon. I told him I imagined he must have read a great number of books to accumulate so much knowledge.

He looked at me through thumb-thick glasses.

—You bet. Yknow, when I was a young man I loved to read. I mean, I *really* loved to read. I always had a book in front of my face. That's why I wear such thick glasses. I read more books than any ten professors, I'll bet. I've read every book there is to be read. You think I'm kidding?

I shrugged neutrally.

—Why should I kid? What a thing to kid about. I read every book in the Hollywood Public Library. I read and read and then one day I couldn't read anymore. I just stopped. Stopped reading novels, philosophies . . . boy, did I got through those books on philosophy! . . . fantasies, criticism, sociologies, anthropologies, mythologies . . . and then I just stopped. I'd had it. I was through with words. They didn't work. They didn't work on the page for me. They didn't tell me anything anymore. They just didn't make any sense to me. You can't understand it, can you? I bet you read all the time and you think that's what life is all about. Well it isn't. Take it from me, from one who knows. No book can tell you about real pain. No book can tell you about the real suffering man inflicts upon himself and other men. Only hints. Everything's after the fact, gone. Ghost stories. I've read them all, yknow. All the books you can think of. Ask me a title, an author. Go ahead. I've read them all. I've lived a lot, yknow. And I finally discovered that only numbers are truth. Numbers, stars, and horses.

He lit another cigarette and I noticed again how his thumb and forefinger were stained dark brown by nicotine.

He told me that when he finished his manuscript—

which was nearly four hundred pages long including charts, diagrams, statistics and graphs—he would publish it himself and sell the book through the mails.

—Could I see it when you've printed it?

—Sure, kid. But you won't understand any of it. Mark my words. As long as you still read books, you won't understand any of it, yknow. But, sure. Why not. What the hell?

I'll show it to you.

•

Our family lives in a 1950-style house in the hills of Richmond, California overlooking neighborhood backyards, urban sprawl, freeways, oil refineries, San Francisco Bay, San Francisco, Marin and Mount Tamalpais.

One day, the neighbors directly below us placed a small black coffee table outside their back door. Later they stacked six tall piles of books upon the table.

It didn't appear that there was anything unusual or significant about this event. My guess was that they were house-painting and wanted the books out of the way of splashed or spilt paint.

The books have remained on the table in the backyard for nearly three months. They have been out there as long as I've been writing this book. They have been rained upon, snowed upon, hailed upon, sun-baked, frost-bit, wind-whipped, even a cat pissed on them. And no one has come back to take them inside. So the table covered with books has become a shrine to a mystery. (In the back of my mind I suspect television.)

Now, every day, I look down into our neighborhood's backyard in hopes that the table and books will be back inside. So far nothing has changed. I suspect it never will.

•

# PART NINE

*1977: was 40*
*2014: am 77*

*appending fragments of 4 decades afterwards after words*

The quest as if to name it.

As if to name it will, for a moment, be enough.

Want to tell, to name, define, fix the known flow, translate.

As if space beyond question is easy when hearing the right combination of words describing what is known.

As if to name it is enough.

How to approach the answer with the question it requires for completion.

We see what our language allows.

This seems clear enough for now.

·

Uw Men wrote: "As a fruit gradually ripening, your time will ripen, and by a natural process your interior and exterior will finally become smoothed out into one whole sheet."

As they are the way, words also get in the way.

That Maine fisherman who told my friend bragging about his way with fish: "Don't tell me, boy, show me."

Translated by Guy Davenport, Heraclitus asked: "How can you hide from what never goes away?"

All that survives are words on paper, fragments

Heraclitus may have written many books or only the one partially surviving in fragments dedicated to Atriums.

We know him as we know Sappho
What broken pages awake in our imagination
Neither to add to nor to subtract
Always somehow to understand
Always somehow to not understand
What is always missing
which never goes away.

•

Before word or its sound. No word, no sound of it, no letters to shape it, letter it. No sound or letters or word. No syllables. No vowels. Consonants. Before letter into word is carved or scraped or brushed into paper or stone or parchment. Before letter into word is marked and then, as notes of music, read and uttered out from behind the eyes into the air shattered by sound. Before word or letter or its sound or sounds. Before.

•

As if to name it.
As if to name it will be, for a moment, enough.

Poets or mystics or prophets desire more.
They want to tell, to name, define, fix the flux known, translate.

As if a peace beyond question comes easily when hearing or seeing the right combination of words defining what's suddenly known.

•

Ask yourself which words you serve.

Which words order your attention?

Those bordered concepts.

Do they lose purpose or meaning to become beyond questioning?

The only book to read when able to read should be a dictionary. Starting from the simplest *Golden Dictionary* and moving along to another and another until one's second decade. They get thicker and denser and there's no end to defining, explaining some of the most basic words we think we know which have a way of expanding rather than contracting, until there often seems no center to meaning.

All else: stories, myths, poems, ideas, lore, should be spoken aloud, sounded, sung, remembered, as you continue to read your expanding bookshelves of dictionaries.

The ritual means only as long as the words mean.

Losing faith is losing a language.

•

Who and when is the poet?
What's in between, what's at work before and after?

•

Every word a tradition, a binding.

Self-rudder, part a path through chaos.

Everything in place when named. Word a face. Even loss of faith in words affirms. Perishable, unable to mean or define. Then play within the music.

How to get past utterances, reiteration of laws, judgment. It is this, it is that, it is so. Author, authority, other, out there. Play within the music, bound to song, the drum, the harp. The struggle with words, mystics and poets. It is known, how to say it, tell it.

What is it to be in cycles of what one is? Even the first time asked, the answer is awake.

How many questions am I awake enough to answer? When I ask myself a question do I listen to its answer?

•

Northrop Frye asks: "Why are belief and disbelief, as ordinarily understood, so often and so intensely anxious and insecure?"

•

When I wonder who's writing my writing, I'll also wonder who reads what I'm writing. Who is there once never the same again ever-present; what moves through words birthing as easily as murdering?

•

A mystery means meanings. It is potential or neutral like a page. The meanings withdrawn like the letters impressed are a rite; each awaits the other as much for continuance as for contemplation. The meaning of a mystery has to do with all the meanings one finds there.

•

Find words of power, words you can fill with their full dimension. Write them as often as possible. Like stone-smashing, see what breaks apart from the core. Watch roots grow.

•

Repetition is one key. Reduction is another. Let repeated words of power merge into a word within a word inside words like a seed; reduce words to word.

Go inside a word; surround yourself with it.

•

An amulet is often the abbreviation of many words, or an amulet is a group of choice words repeated within a formal design like a square or circle or triangle.

Paper is one substance to mark them on, also parchment or canvas or sand or silk or silver or ivory or tin. There are no specific tools for creation except those that work best. The power you seek is within. Like a poem, an amulet is a creative act. Like all ongoing openings of the imagination there need be no fixed form; like snowflakes, the structure and content of your amulet depends on your ability to extend yourself within creation.

•

Study the formal urgency of amulets from all cultures. Develop your own style of writing, calligraphy, your own imprint. Prepare yourself. Take your words of power seriously. Focus your form into each mark, letter, word. Impregnate them. They are suns and stars and snowflakes. They are molecules.

•

Experiment with writing other alphabets.

Write automatically in instantly invented Greek, Suzerain, Chinese, Cro-Magnon, Egyptian. Study, involve yourself with (and within) pictograms, ideograms, hieroglyphs, without necessarily knowing their meanings or the logic of their forms.

•

The word emerging is turned into a code. The code is constantly changing.

The mystery of language is that no one understands it.

•

We live in a four-cornered world. We live on the page, on the screen.

We are walking books, alphabets, poems; blinking into the page of light, I make my black marks.

•

A presence also a present, a gift. Something we often make into someone, i.e., an angel or muse, a voice or a figure, either seen within or beyond. An appearance adhering to no fixed duration. Engaging as a child's invisible companion or a sudden unseen other another crazed one yells at striding furiously down lunch-hour streets.

"The daemon has foresight,
the psyche is blind and time bound"

What was complete is fragmented into words remembering it. Face it. A presence, a present presents, gives.

"Angel" from the Greek *angelos*, angels as translation from the Hebrew *malakh*, a messenger. A form, a resemblance, a figure. A voice or melody within.

•

As God translates it for the angel into tones of essence sensible to hold in memory, angel in turn translates it for the human translating into the poem of prophecy announced to those assembled translating.

"Translate" suggests a range of complex maneuvers excluding, including, imposing, supposing. And who "gets" the message "gives" it to others who shape into words others will understand (or "get" it). The same never the same.

•

"A gift from the gods." From the beginning, inspired insight attributed as a gift or message from another entity, one from a higher plane, a spiritual reality parallel with our earthly, shadow-casting, gravity—enjambed reality.

"Inspiration," the god or goddess breathing vision through you, and what before was broken in a moment seems complete.

•

Dhirgatamas, Hindu philosopher-poet, millennia ago asked

"I ask you: What is the ultimate limit of the earth?
I ask you: What is the central point of the Universe?
I ask you: What is the semen of the cosmic horse?
I ask you: What is the ultimate dwelling of Language?"

•

Who is in each word your breath inspires?

•

"The poet makes poetry with the poetry that is given to him in advance," wrote Max Picard.

•

Speech is the best show man puts on. It is his own "act" on the stage of evolution, in which he comes before the cosmic backdrop and really "does his stuff." But we suspect the watching Gods perceive that the order in which his amazing set of tricks builds up to a great climax has been stolen from the Universe! The idea, entirely unfamiliar to the modern world, that nature and language are inwardly akin, was for ages well known to various high cultures whose historical continuity on the earth has been enormously longer than that of Western European culture.

—Benjamin Lee Whorf (1942)

•

What moments are "beyond words"?

•

The page as a creation myth.

Its white form embodying light and similar (and continuous) concepts of higher knowledge. Its light linked to the Sun and Moon, universal in creation myths. Light is to see and the page is a space where words are placed to look at in order to see what is either beyond or within or in front of us, or all of it at once.

The page or piece of paper, analogous to beginnings, tabula rasa, mystic pad. The page or piece of paper, a veil taken from a tree.

Its white the light of Yang, male element, creator; whereas the letters and words the become are black, Yin, feminine, receiver, incubator of beginnings.

•

Consider the shape of a page. Why square instead of round? A basic question with I'm sure rather elemental answers. On the surface, we're walking through walls when we turn a page. Do we read or enter a book? Do we remember it as each of its pages, or do we walk away from it with our own book in our memory?

•

Edmond Jabès writes: "And I realized that to be a writer is to be a Jew in a certain way, it's to live a certain Jewish condition, separated, exiled. And that the problems that are posed to Judaism are posed regularly to the writer because the Jew has nothing but his book that he has to force himself to read and to understand. Whence all the commentaries of the book. Whence the obsessions with what's been written. Not just what's been written, but with what conceals what's been written. What must be read. As if there was a book hiding another book from me. And there too I draw a reference to the writer, because I deeply believe that each writer carries a book in him that he will never do. All the books he writes try to approach it. And if he never does this book, it's because if he managed to, he wouldn't write anymore. Because this be the book. And if it's feasible, it's because our speech is not definitive. It's a speech made up of changes. We cannot express ourselves in a total manner, only by small steps."

•

Again: to consider a book, not only its shape, but how the printed pages are bound, to the left, allowing us two pages at a time. Left to center, page one; center to right, page two, across each slight hill we read like a skier.

•

Pay attention. Pay attention to everything. To nothing. What's there? Describe what isn't with as much focus as what is. Focus all at once. Detail the seen, heard, felt. Pay attention to paying attention. Note everything down. What people say. The banter of small and big talk. What's being said? What's unsaid? Read faces, gestures.

Have a fast pen or pencil or gizmo to track where you are in that moment to moment. Watch don't wait. Note it with clarity.

•

For some the learning of literacy is entering a particular sphere of institutional culture, for others it happens in the home sphere as preparation for entering institutional culture. Each and every aspect of alphabetic literacy represents visible and invisible social values and forms. (Though it's possible to participate in market culture by being unable to read, being "functionally illiterate," you're often damaged by your socially enforced "disability.")

•

Let me tell you how I learned to read since it's only fair that you get a sense of my contradictions. Both parents read to me and my sisters, but I remember my mother did most of the reading out of discarded library books they'd bought at rummage sales. I remember the "thinness" of the books she read from: the thick library buckram bindings, gold stamping of titles and authors on the spine, the deep black imprint of large round type on each page somewhat yellowed by use and time. It was a book of fairy tales, maybe Grimm or Andersen. Her act of translating those glyphs from that inexplicable square shape that fanned open. Also sitting close together in a well-broken-in (some would say broken-down) stuffed easy chair bathed in a golden light filtered through a dusty fluted lampshade surrounding the floor-standing lamp. All this "gold" could be memory's patina turning time flashbacks into sepia-toned snapshots.

My mother said I taught myself to read when I was four or five by naming letters wherever I saw them—on billboards, bookspines, newspapers, magazines—A, B, C, etc.—just letters, not the words they combined to turn into. Somehow soon letters locked into words and I began poring over kid books, ultimately graduating to a library card that a family friend, the local librarian, let me have since I was under age—I could barely write or print my name, but could read and wanted to read everything.

I had a red metal wagon I'd drag to the library and fill with books from the kids' section which I'd read one at a time and then, the next day, bring them back and load up the wagon with more until I'd read all of them and started edging into the enormous adult stacks. Then kicking and screaming to kindergarten. I'd become an avid reader—"voracious" fits too.

•

Our culture, our histories, start in utterance of sound, a creating word announcing reality, boundaries, the limits of spirit, imagination and art which then struggle to serve and extend those limits.

We're word-bound. The words along with the biological creation alphabet, holds us to our situation, our place in each moment. The words or their absence corner and surround our lives with purpose and futility.

•

Wanting words on the page to say more than they say.

Wanting words on the page to say exactly what they say.

An attempted eternity. Bones are not enough. A civilization becomes known only through its records, its notations, the marks of seen and unseen reality on tools or bowls or scrolls. Not wanting to forget or be forgotten, we make our marks and invest in them the potency to transcend and somehow be understood. Through the beginning of spoken language to the development of written language, everyone thought their language to be the only language, their words the only words connected to what they described. The early Greeks couldn't understand a conquered tribe's speech. It sounded like *bar-bar*, hence the word "barbarian."

•

Prophet: Greek: Speaking before (an event); proclaimer, spokesman; interpreter for gods, goddesses and oracles; "pro"—before; "phone"—to say.

Poet: Greek: "maker" from "poetess," "poison"—to make, create.

Seer: a prophet; a clairvoyant; Middle English—from "seen," "to see."

Fool: Latin: folios: "bellows," "bag" or "ball inflated with air"; cf. "windbag."

•

William Blake wrote in *There Is No Natural Religion*:

"If it were not for the Poetic or Prophetic character the Philosophic & Experimental would soon be at the ratio of all things, & stand still unable to do other than repeat the same dull round over again."

Later he writes: "The desire of Man being Infinite the possession is infinite & himself Infinite."

Application. He who sees the Infinite in all things sees God. He who sees the Ratio only sees himself only.

Therefore God becomes as we are, that we may be as he is.

•

Eleazar of Worms, kabbalist of the 12th/13th centuries, wrote:

"The Creator is purely intelligible and yet no creature of this world has heard His Voice. The word leaves the mouth of His Glory as an impression of a word living creatures cannot receive the complete discourse all at once, but only little by little, as one spreads out coins, piece after piece."

•

Then I asked: does a firm persuasion that a thing is so, make it so?

He replied. All poets believe that it does, & in ages of imagination this firm persuasion removes mountains; but many are not capable of a firm persuasion of anything.

—William Blake, *Marriage of Heaven & Hell.*

•

In Plato's *Apology*: "I soon found that it is not by wisdom that the poets create their works, but by a certain natural power and by inspiration, like soothsayers and prophets, who say many fine things, but who understand nothing of what they say."

•

I distrust hierarchies: they invariably explain (impose) the same image of power, yet I'm also aware of (and susceptible to) their fascination. They offer easy ordering to store in memory; they give position in times of upheaval; they offer the enclosure of form as barrier against intimations of chaos, disorder, formlessness. They withhold and confine; they fetishize the binary into a perpetual them/us, weak/strong rationale not even mysticism can shake off or break through.

Power excludes, is exclusive. Each floor of the tower has its own king who "answers" to those kings above him (literally) to all those "under" him. Power implies above, the top. Boss, king, star, etc. Maybe at the top of the tower is the omnipotent CEO sitting at his immense and almost empty desk.

Behind him is an enormous window where the sky is perpetually blue and the outline of condos, high rises, and corporate kingdoms creates a silent affirmation of hubris incarnate. He is alone. No need to think, plan, or scheme. Or dream.

Happily empty.

•

After all these years and only for this moment—"No ideas but in things"—rings clear, imperative.  Bring image, color, make particular.  What's there, outside, to see it.  Not the idea-words maelstrom hurricane-in-head Niagara falling, roaring away all other music, taking ideas down its thunder drop like all those other clowns in barrels.

•

Father's ghost gifted with Maugham's *Writer's Note Book* from mother. She turns to me, "You should read this," which I try to but never finish. Kept reading book after book looking for one that had my "orders" in it.

•

I still want to know "who" writes when writing is being written.

•

We noun, announce, pronounce, flounce, flaunt nouns.

Nun nouns. Cowl them, girt them, black and white them, back and forth, whose book is holy, whose page sacred black and white; some texts red with speaking seeing blood.

We noun, we numb, succumb to name, to naming, display, replay numb nouns where power's assumed to be stored, adored in its divisions.

King Dumb above us, under His thumb. He but half and his half death darkens our garden day and night.

Flipbook rapid-fire cuts allow an image a second too fast for brain to name.

"It's so nice out in the garden, I wish you could go out there and see it," she says. I tell her I'll take her word for it. The garden, the word, for it, for her.

It's never clear who is (or if anyone is) dictating what I transcribe. Monumental signs and letters ascend ancient pillars, immense stone pages, counting, declaring song, history, partial, official, granite, which if it remains, remains as fact.

The song, the story, remembered in words inscribed, enscrolled, encoded, entrusted, stored, silent, breathless, entombed.

•

Homer, blind singer of story we never hear as he never saw nor wrote a word.

•

The drama of our time is the coming of all men into one fate, "the dream of everyone, everywhere." The fate or dream is the fate of more than mankind. Our secret Adam is written now in the script of the primal cell. We have gone beyond the reality of the incomparable nation or race, the incomparable Jehovah in the shape of a man, the incomparable Book or Vision, the incomparable species, in which identity might hold and defend its boundaries against an alien territory. All things have come now into their comparisons. But these comparisons are the correspondence that haunted Paracelsus, who saw also that the key to man's nature was hidden in the larger nature.

—Robert Duncan: "Rites of Participation"

•

Torlino, an old Navajo priest, prepares to tell the Navajo Creation Myth to an anthropologist:

I am ashamed before the earth;
I am ashamed before the heavens;
I am ashamed before the dawn;
I am ashamed before the evening twilight;
I am ashamed before the blue sky;
I am ashamed before the sun.
*I am ashamed before that standing within me which speaks with me.*
Some of these things are always looking at me.
I am never out of sight.
Therefore I must tell the truth.
*I hold my word tight to my breast.*

•

77 now and you'd think I'd know more not less than when I wrote this book. Not true. Time adds, subtracts, edits, obliterates certainty, and renews a primary sense of starting all over again, constantly beginning.

•

I'm grateful to Kenneth Rexroth for telling me to "watch out for the embrace," referring to the tragic deaths of Dylan Thomas & Jack Kerouac—and many other writers & artists suicided by society's dazzle blaze and bafflement with stars, fame. The fans' hunger is to absorb and devour their imaginary others.

•

Humans get away from humans.

They'll go to the mountains or the woods or the waters.

To "commune" with nature & perhaps be restored or mended

or "get things together."

We "go" to nature but what do we return to?

•

In the blues (though not necessarily elsewhere) black women express power & grief equally with black men.

What's possible for Blind Blake to sing is no less possible for Ma Rainey.

Men & women sing of conquest or defeat on equal ground with equal authority.

African song tradition is collective, plural; self inseparable from tribe.

Here in high or low arts, self is subject & author.

Self apart, detached, broken off (or cast away) from a "wholeness" impossible to imagine wholly.

•

Why is poetry?

Most of us know what it is, but *why* is it, how did it happen?

These talks are a preliminary attempt to trace the unfolding biography of poetry, its roots of being.

Begin at the beginning: pulse, tone, breath, sound—all awake in utero: mother's heartbeat, inside and outside sounds entering into the embryo's water world.

•

### Mrs. White at Night School

Mrs. White is in New York. She is at her friend's house.

Yesterday Mrs. White went to night school with her friend. She saw men and women there. She saw the teacher.

The teacher sent a man to the library. The woman in the library gave a book to this man. The woman said, "Here is a book for Mrs. White."

---

NEW WORDS: at with which

---

**Some books that have inspired & incited my poetic adventures:**

Ezra Pound. *ABC of Reading* (also EP's version of Ernest Fennelosa's *The Chinese Character as a Written Medium*).

Henry Miller. *The Books in My Life*, also *Time of the Assassins* (on Rimbaud).

Susan Howe. *My Emily Dickinson*.

Kenneth Koch. *Dreams, Wishes, and Lies*.

William Carlos Williams. *I Wanted to Write a Poem: The Autobiography of the Works of a Poet*.

Kenneth Rexroth. *Classics Revisited*.

Lew Welch. *How I Work as a Poet*.

Lawrence Ferlinghetti. *Poetry as an Insurgent Art*.

*Pages  Source*

17 *Pre-Columbian Literature of Mexico* by Miguel León-Portilla. University of Oklahoma Press, 1969.

19 *The Oxford Dictionary of Nursery Rhymes*, edited by Iona and Peter Opie. Oxford University Press, 1951.

22 *The Dancing Chimpanzee: A study of the origin of primitve music* by Leonard Williams. W.W. Norton, New York, 1967.

23 *Corpus Hermeticum*, edited and translated by W. Scott. Oxford University Press, 1924–1926.

25 *The Netsilik Eskimos* by Knut Rasmussen. Copenhagen, 1931.

26 *Dieu d'Eau* by Marcel Griaule. Paris, 1948.

27 *Munfu* by Janheinz Jahn (translated by Marjorie Grene). Grove Press, New York, 1961.

31–32 *The Alphabet: A key to the history of mankind* by David Diringer. Philosophical Library, New York, 1948; revised and expanded edition published by Funk and Wagnalls, New York, 1968. Other books by Professor Diringer of interest are: *Writing: Its Origins and Early History* (Thames and Hudson, London, 1962) and *The Illuminated Book* (Praeger, New York, 1967).

33 *Barddas; or, a collection of original documents illustrative of the Theology, Wisdom and Usages of the Bardo-Druidic System of the Isle of Britain*, edited and translated by J. Williams (Ab Ithel). Bernard Quaritch, London, 1874.

34–35 See listing for page 27.

36 *Gypsy Sorcery and Fortune Telling* by C.G. Leiand. University Books, New Hyde Park, 1963.

37 *Leaves of Grass* by Walt Whitman. From Whitman's introduction to the first edition, 1855. The best edition is edited by Malcolm Cowley, published by Viking Press, New York, 1959.

38–39 *Dictionary of Classical Antiquities* by Oskar Seyffert, revised and edited, with additions, by Henry Nettleship and J.E. Sandys. Meridian Books, New York, 1963.

40 The new standard edition of Blake is *The Poetry and Prose of William Blake*, edited by David V. Erdman, commentary by Harold Bloom. Doubleday and Company, Garden City, 1965. Another version of this statement appears at the end of *A Vision of the Last Judgment* (1810): "What it will be Questioned When the Sun rises do you not see a round Disk of fire somewhat like a Guinea O no no I see an Innumerable company of the Heavenly host crying

Holy Holy Holy is the Lord God Almighty I question not my Corporeal or Vegetative Eye any more than I would Question a Window concerning a Sight I look thro it & not with."

41 *The Heads of the Town up to the Aether* by Jack Spicer. Auerhahn Press, San Francisco, 1962; reprinted in *The Collected Books of Jack Spicer*, edited by Robin Blaser (Black Sparrow Press, Los Angeles, 1975).

42 *Towards a Happy Solstice, Mine Yours Everybody* by John Brandi. Christopher's Books/Tree Books, Santa Barbara, 1971.

45 Same listing as page 33.

55 *Souvenir Book of Calypsoes Composed and Sung by Singers at The Young Brigade*, compiled by Lord Melody. Nu-way, Trinidad, n.d.

58 Same listing as page 33.

59 *The American Indians and Their Music* by Frances Densmore. The Woman's Press, New York, 1926.

60 *A Dictionary of Angels*, edited and compiled by Gustav Davidson. Free Press, New York, 1967.

62 *Le livre de questions* by Edmond Jabès. Éditions Gallimard, Paris, 1963. Translated by Rosmarie Waldrop. Two books by Jabès are now available in English: *Elya,* translated by Rosmarie Waldrop (Tree Books, Berkeley, 1973) and *The Book of Questions*, translated by Rosmarie Waldrop (Wesleyan University Press, Middletown, Connecticut, 1976).

65 *Music and Imagination* by Aaron Copland. Harvard University Press, Cambridge, 1952.

67 "More Ingredients" by Whitney Balliett in *The New Yorker,* August 12, 1972, subsequently reprinted in *Alec Wilder and His Friends: The words and sounds of Marian McPartland, Mabel Mercer, Marie Marcus, Bobby Hackett, Tony Bennett, Ruby Braff, Bob and Ray, Blossom Dearie and Alec Wilder* (Houghton Mifflin, Boston, 1974).

68–69 *The San Francisco Poets*, edited by David Meltzer. Ballantine Books, New York, 1971; reprinted as *Golden Gate: Interviews with 5 San Francisco poets* (Wingbow Press, Berkeley, 1976).

91 *The Book of Tea* by Kakuzo Okakura. Originally published in 1906, reprinted by Dover Publications, Incorporated, New York, 1964.

94 See listing for page 37.

98 *Shamanism: Archaic techniques of ecstasy* by Mircea Eliade. Princeton University Press (Bollingen Series), Princeton, 1964.

99 From Blake's *The Marriage of Heaven and Hell.* See listing for page 40.

100 "Notes on Smack" by Clark Coolidge in *Smack* by Tom Clark. Black Sparrow Press, Los Angeles, 1972.

125 See listing for page 33.

140 *Conversations with Igor Stravinsky* by Robert Craft. Doubleday and Company, Garden City, 1958.

158 *The Interior and Exterior in Zen Buddhism* by Toshihiko Izutsu. Spring Publications, Dallas, Texas, 1984.

164 *The Great Code: The Bible and Literature* in Collected Works of Northrop Frye, v. 19, edited by Alvin A. Lee. University of Toronto, Toronto, 2006.

176 *Meditations Through the Rig Veda: Four-Dimensional Man* by Antonio T. DeNicolás. iUniverse, Lincoln, Nebraska, 2003.

178 *Man and Language* by Max Picard. Forgotten Books, London, 2013.

179 *Language, Thought, and Reality: Selected Writings of Benjamin Lee Whorf.* M.I.T. Press, Cambridge, 1956. [p249.]

183 *Writing at Risk: Interviews in Paris with Uncommon Writers* by Jason Weiss. University of Iowa Press, Iowa City, 1991.

194 From Blake's *The Marriage of Heaven and Hell.* See listing for page 40.

202 *A Selected Prose* by Robert Duncan, edited by Robert J. Berthoff. New Directions, New York, 1995. [p97]

203 *The Winged Serpent: American Indian Prose and Poetry*, edited by Margot Astrov. Beacon Press, Boston, 1946, 1974. [p2]

A poet at age 11, David Meltzer began his literary career during the Beat heyday in San Francisco and early on took his poetry to jazz for improv wonders, with which he continues to astound listeners today. He is the author of many volumes of poetry, including *The Clown, The Process, Arrows: Selected Poetry, 1957–1992, No Eyes: Lester Young, Beat Thing, David's Copy*, and *When I Was A Poet*, which was published by City Lights as #60 in the Pocket Poets Series. Meltzer has edited numerous anthologies, such as *Reading Jazz, Writing Jazz*, and *San Francisco Beat: Talking with the Poets*. He was also the lead singer and guitarist of the psychedelic folk-rock group Serpent Power. He taught in the Humanities and graduate Poetics programs at New College of California in San Francisco for 30 years. He is now performing in and around the Bay Area with his wife, poet Julie Rogers.